# HOW I MET MY MAN

*And*

# HOW YOU CAN MEET YOURS

*by*

Delissa Needham

**Copyright © 2022 by Delissa Needham**

All rights reserved. No part of this publication may be reproduced, distributed, or transmitted in any form or by any means, including photocopying, recording, or other electronic or mechanical methods, without the prior written permission of the publisher, except in the case of brief quotations embodied in critical reviews and certain other non-commercial uses permitted by copyright law.

Edited by Vicky Manduca

Cover Design by Prudence Makhura

Hardcover ISBN: 9798363112102

Paperback ISBN: 9798363767159

*"How to meet the perfect man
if you don't have my phone number"*

# Cosmo Landesman

*for my lovely friend Sandra*
*naughty, graceful, poised, creative and fun. I miss you.*


*With thanks to my wonderful friend,*
*Dr Rita Rakus who inspired this book.*


*A big thank you to Vicky for her editing and encouragement.*

*Also thanks to the very special Paul Hayes*

# Foreword

Looking for love online is not for everyone. This book is.

When a friend asked me to help him find a girlfriend it seemed like a fun thing to do. He didn't want to use dating sites, or introduction agencies, but nor did he want to leave something so important to chance. He knew what he wanted so we just needed a plan of action. One that would increase his prospects. The result of our focussed planning is that he's now married and has two sons.

You may well meet someone by chance, but can you really wait for it to happen? It could take too long. The opportunities diminish as we get older. We go out less, and we find that not everyone in the room is in the 'mating game' anymore. So how do you improve your 'chances'. How do you increase the possibilities? Where do you go? Where do you look? What do you do? These are questions single women ask me all the time.

## How do you get what you want? How do you meet a man?

The answer is that you need to take a different approach. Creating and producing dating shows for TV means I've learnt a thing or two, especially about the science of attraction and gender behaviour. And of course I have my own way of doing things. Looking for love online is not how I go about meeting a man. I did once try. I was given free membership from the dating show I was producing, and so I posted a photo of me standing in my kitchen next to my fridge. One man replied by asking me how much for the fridge? He was funny, but I already knew him from when we'd met at a party two years earlier. That had been much more fun way of meeting him. I prefer the real-world approach, but you need to know where to go. You need a focussed, planned "get out there and get on with it" approach. Then, at the very least, you'll have a good time.

*How I Met My Man* came from a conversation I had with my friend Rita Rakus when we were swapping our favourite stories on how couples had met. I decided to include some in this book, so you don't just hear the message from me. The stories are reminders that love can happen anywhere, anytime, and anyhow. It's such wonderful serendipity when two people meet. How does it happen that they find themselves in the right place at the right time, and somehow manage to collide in this big world with someone who will become their world? It's happened to me. Like the time I fell in love with the man who came to buy my car. How random is that? Or the new

vi

boyfriend I met after I pulled into a busy road and managed to get my old banger connected with the side of his smart Jag. How did that ugly situation turn around? Even odder, the soon to be boyfriend I met on the first floor of the Eiffel Tower. I was unable to move, immobilised by vertigo and clutching the wall with my eyes shut when I heard someone ask if I was alright. He was a handsome Parisian smelling delightfully of Gauloise and cologne and offering me a steady hand so I could let go of the wall. It was definitely love at first height.

These are all meetings that happened quite by chance, and in the pages of this book you will find practical advice on how to give chance a helping hand. This is how you too can meet your man.

# Contents

FOREWORD ..................................................................... v
INTRODUCTION ............................................................. 1

## PART 1: YOU FIRST. THE FOUR MOST IMPORTANT THINGS. ............................................. 9

ARE YOU READY TO MEET A NEW MAN? ........ 11
LET'S START WITH HAPPINESS. ....................... 24
DO YOU NEED HELP WITH YOUR SELF CONFIDENCE? .................................................... 34
WHAT'S TROUBLING YOU? WHY SORTING YOUR MIND IS SUCH AN IMPORTANT FIRST STEP. ......... 47

## PART 2: WHAT YOU NEED TO KNOW ............... 55

WHAT MEN WANT AND WHAT WOMEN WANT .. 57
THE POWER OF CHEMISTRY. SMELL AND HOW IT WORKS FOR YOU. ........................................... 70
STOP MAKING THE WRONG LISTS AND START MAKING THE RIGHT ONES. ................................ 78
BE FOCUSSED BUT BE OPEN ............................. 88

## PART 3: STRATEGIC THINKING ........................ 97

WHERE TO LOOK. ............................................... 99
HOW TO NETWORK FOR DATING. ................... 111

WHAT DO YOU WANT? REALLY, REALLY WANT? ...................................................................... 115

HOW TO LOOK GOOD AND THE PLEASURE OF MEETING NEW PEOPLE. .............................................. 123

HOW TO GET IN THE RIGHT ROOM. ................... 132

RESEARCH IS YOUR BEST DATING FRIEND ...... 142

USING THE INTERNET FOR DATING. ................... 147

**PART 4: THINK YES!** ................................................. **159**

KNOCK OFF THE CORNERS. ................................. 161

THINK YOU WILL AND YOU WILL. ...................... 170

DATING IN THE REAL WORLD IS FUN. ............... 178

RECAP: LET'S GO OVER THAT AGAIN. ................ 179

**PART 5: AND FINALLY…** ........................................ **189**

FOR THE 35's AND UNDER ................................. 191

STUFF FOR YOU TO THINK ABOUT ................... 199

# Introduction

Love is such an important part of a happy life, yet we have such a haphazard way of finding it. At the heart of all our hopes for love is that we will be in the right place at the right time; that a sliding door moment will happen. Certainly, it's the serendipity of love that makes it so special when it happens. It's why couples always remember how they met. Very often they were just in the right place at the right time. And so passively, probably lazily, and probably because of the many romantic stories we are brought up with, we wait, and we hope that love will find us. We probably give more attention to finding Ottolenghi ingredients than we do to finding love. When we want to get fit, we are much more organised. We can hire a personal trainer or join a gym. If we need help with depression, we see a therapist. We proactively network to make our business work or consult a stylist to help us choose the right look. So should we treat love so very differently? Why don't we hire love coaches to help find love? Someone to help focus and encourage you and someone to strategize for you. Work out where you need to be and what you need to do so that you stand more chance of being in the right place at the right time. You are probably reading this book because that serendipity is taking its sweet time and you've decided it's time to give chance a helping hand. You may well have weighed up your odds and concluded you need help. That's a good start. So now you need a Love Coach. I hope this book will be your own Love Coach.

Deciding that you need to focus on finding love is the first step on the journey. Now you need to work out what you want and how you will find it. The aim of this book is to help you do that. It's time to stop trying the hopeless tried and failed routes. It's time instead to think outside the box armed with a plan of action based on who you are and what you would like.

I help many women with one-to-one coaching, many of whom are divorced or widowed. Like them, many of you will have tried online dating agencies or introduction agencies and have been disappointed at best and scammed at worst. It makes me furious that many women are viewed as targets just because they want to be loved and find partners in life. I hope my book will show you a new and more fun approach.

*How I Met My Man* is my step-by-step strategy. Its practical advice, guidance, tips, and encouragement help you to adopt a more focussed approach to finding the right match. In this book you will find useful research particularly on gender behaviour as well as research gathered from many different sources to support you. There are chapters on how to look and where to look. The guidance and tips on how to find love are followed by heart-warming and true stories to remind you how wonderful it is to meet the right person. All the stories in *How I Met My Man* are about people who fell crazily and hopelessly in love. None of these stories are about people who met someone either online or by an introduction agency. I believe the best way to find love is to go and look for it – armed with a healthy physical and mental outlook, and a thought-out strategy. Most of all you will enjoy yourself in the process. I doubt the same can be said for the repetitive strain injury you'll get from scrolling countless websites looking for love.

Online dating sites involve looking at endless images and trying to guess the real personality between the lines of the blurb. If you are picking someone out based on a nice smile or attractive eyes, then surely my neighbour's Bengal cat is in with a chance! Or you wait for the weird algorithms to do their thing. After a few months of this you realise the only 'fit man' knocking on your door is delivering parcels. A part of the reason this process fails is that we don't stop and think first about the reality of who we are and what we want. In a later chapter you can examine your realistic approach – it's crucial thinking in your strategy.

Some of my dating clients have been down the route of the introduction agency. You hand over a fee (sometimes five figure sums) in the belief that an agency expert who first met you half an hour ago can know you well enough to match you up to the right partner for life. Many of my dating clients have found the introduction method to be disappointing, demoralising, and expensive with no guaranteed outcome.

Introducing two single people is a method I refuse to use with my clients. Even if I may think there's a remote possibility of success by introducing two people – I don't do it.

It's an unnatural process right from the start and it creates discomfort for everyone. No outside person can really tell what will work between two people - it's a complete mystery. What makes two people fall in love? You walk into a party, lock eyes across a plate of salmon twirls and suddenly there it is – the magic of love. You listed your ideal woman as a tall brunette, but you're transfixed by this curvy blonde you could fit in an egg cup! You dream of a hunky bodybuilder, but the man you can't stop listening to couldn't bench-press a peanut. You don't know if he likes opera, rare burgundy or pina coladas at sunset. You don't know anything other than you feel like you could listen to this person for ever and ever. Whatever that intangible magic is that fires love, it doesn't happen via a computer. Falling in love is an unpredictable, exciting, and romantic adventure.

It is likely you are in the 40+ age group of singles. This is the largest, most neglected group of women across the globe when it comes to the dating scene. These are a group of women who are divorced, widowed or have been wed to their careers and quite naturally you want to find someone special to share the rest of your life with. It's a daunting prospect but *How I Met My Man* will help you become more confident, meet more men, and increase your opportunities of finding love. All it takes is a little re-thinking, some subtle tweaking and directing your actions in a way that's more focussed.

How do I have this knowledge? I've created and produced several television shows on dating for ITV, Channel 5, Living Channel and C4 and as an agony aunt I've answered questions on love and helped countless numbers of singles to meet that special somebody. Now it's your turn. Together we'll build that plan of action.

I've always been curious about how couples originally met, so I always ask and consequently over the years, I've collected some amazing stories. What fascinates me is that very often the couple still view their love through the lens of that first time they met. This is the sliding doors moment that gives us hope. Proof we should never give up – you really don't know what could happen and when. The crucial tip is, always be ready. Love can happen <u>anywhere</u>, anytime, and anyhow. That's what's so wonderfully serendipitous about it. However, a little judicious planning can help get you there faster. How two people meet is a huge part of their shared romantic story - it kick-starts their love and shadows how the rest of it pans out. Here's a story I love.

## Lauren 55

I met my husband 30 years ago on a stairwell in a building off Charlotte Street in London.

It was hate at first sight.

Like Doris Day and Rock Hudson in Pillow Talk. We were like the worst of romantic comedies. From *Gone with the Wind* to *Pride and Prejudice*, doesn't every great love story have the same theme? Hate turns to love - it's probably a thin line anyway.

What were my first words to him?

*"I'd like a pot of tea and Marmite on toast"*.

And what were his first words to me? This man who would eventually be my loving partner for the next 30 years?

*"Sod off"*.

I was the big shot client – 'The Money'. It was my company that had brought its huge account to this business, so when I passed what I thought was the company 'office boy/dogsbody' on the stairwell I put in my breakfast order. Big mistake!!! Chris was the Chief Engineer. Why is that so significant? Because he is the one person in the company you really, really need to be nice to. When the equipment breaks down, he's the one to help you get back on track to meet a pressing deadline. And of course, it did break down. So you can imagine how I felt when I rang for assistance and Chris came through the door. When I look back now, I wonder how two people could have been more different. He's from Glasgow and I'm from Henley.

But over the next two months it was the run up to Christmas so we ended up at the same company parties. How did it turn around? It just did. Perhaps when two people instantly dislike or despise each other there is only one way it can go.

\*\*\*

Often couples can still recall the tiniest of details of that first meeting, even when it was decades ago.

## Julie 59

I can remember exactly what I was wearing when I first met Charlie. I was strolling down the Kings Road in Chelsea, in a peasant style dress and cowboy boots. My friend, Peter, was sitting outside at a table with another man and he saw me and waved me over. The other diner was Charlie. I can't to this day tell you what Peter was wearing but I do remember exactly Charlie's face, his smile and how immaculately he was dressed and his upright posture. He was wearing a tailored suit in a beautiful cloth with a matching silk tie. My grandfather was a tailor - he dressed many of the aristocracy and professionals such as lawyers and other businessmen. So when I first saw Charlie, I immediately clocked the suit. Opposites we were not. We had a mutual appreciation for style even if mine was a bit rough that day. But the thing I most remember is that when Charlie and I started talking there was no one else at the table. Just the two of us. He left for Boston, USA that afternoon but when he came back five weeks later, he rang me, and we went out to dinner. It was his birthday. Every year since then, we have gone to the same restaurant on the same night for nearly 25 years. I know I was walking down the right street at the right time, but I think, and I know, that if we hadn't met then, somehow, somewhere we would still have met. We were meant to be together.

\*\*\*

Why would you swap the possibility of a romantic beginning such as that for picking a photo out of an internet line up? Online dating couldn't be more unromantic. A cold, desperate and calculated start riddled with more concealment, trickery and masquerading than a Shakespearean comedy. I prefer traditional, more romantic methods of running into love. I leave the house expecting it to happen. And it has happened - in the strangest ways in the strangest, most unexpected of places. I'd like to help more people to do the same.

The tips inside this book will help you to form a strategy that works for you – one that will help you locate the man you are looking for. No more wasted opportunities. There are so many ways to find love if only you looked in the right places. You need to know what to do and how. *How I Met My Man* will help you create a plan of action, a clear strategy and provide you with a tool kit.

# PART 1:
# YOU FIRST.
# THE FOUR MOST
# IMPORTANT
# THINGS.

## *Chapter One*

# ARE YOU READY TO MEET A NEW MAN?

Really ready?

So you want to meet a man? Do you want one to love and marry, or one to keep in the potting shed and bring out when the bills need paying. Are you absolutely sure you want one? They're very simple, men overall. Wouldn't you rather have a cat, a dog or even a gerbil (they only live for two years, so when it's 6 inches underground you can move onto a goldfish).

Ok, so if you're sure, then this book is your step-by-step guide, but you are going to have to do things differently. Stop doing the things you normally do and get ready to try a more focussed method. When I say step out of your comfort zone, I'm not talking about the shop floor that sells slippers. Following my strategy to finding a new man involves having a lot of fun but it also means taking a few planned risks.

*How I Met My Man and How You Can Meet Yours*

So my guess is that as you are single then you are either widowed, divorced, or just not jumped the fence yet. If widowed or divorced, then there's some good news. You have a better chance of getting married again than previous generations where finding another husband was highly unlikely. Travel is easier and the growth of the internet has allowed more connections to be made, more quickly than ever before.

Advances in health mean that people are living for longer and advances in beauty treatments mean we don't have to look like we've been living for longer. It's only natural and to be expected that we all still want a partner to be with. Age no longer has a bearing on that. Increasing income for women allows for all kinds of self-improvement. Women are actively fighting old age, cramming their lives with wonderful things and that includes a man to share it with.

Just look at the figures and you'll realise what's powering the search for someone to share life with. In the UK, it has been estimated by the Innovation Foundation, Nesta, that the spending power of the 'silver economy' will grow from £79 billion to £127 billion by 2030. In the North of England alone there are four million people aged between 50-74 with an annual purchasing power of £1.5 billion. Euromonitor forecasts that the global spending power of those aged 60 and above will almost double from the $8 trillion they spent in 2010, to reach $15tn by 2020.

The future is bright with promise. Now all we have to do is focus. But first, let's look at where you are right now.

It's scary being single, isn't it?

In today's busy world it feels like floating around on a raft on the large lake of life. Friends and family have their own rafts. Everyone is floating around on their own raft occasionally connecting but most often busy with their own splish splosh world. Perhaps you did have someone on your raft but they fell off, or they swam off, or you threw them off, or maybe you've always piloted this raft on your own. You are maybe 45, 55, 60 or even 70+, but importantly you're fed up watching the sunset from your raft all on your tod. Lordy it's boring. You'd like to sit on the edge of the raft and have someone to dangle your toes in the water with. Someone to share a bit of the paddling. Someone to laugh with, to talk with, to love with. Someone to fall in the water with.

Ok so enough of the raft analogy …..

So, what do you do?

All I'm asking of you in this chapter is that you affirm to yourself that you definitely want to meet a man and that you are prepared to try a calculated adventure to make sure that happens. Aspirations are one thing – but actually taking the steps to achieve a goal is the only way to succeed. We've all been there. You should see me come the New Year. Dusting off the designer trainers, pulling on the expensive new kit, choosing the perfect playlist, and finally setting off down the country track with that wonderful sense of the 'freedom of the road'. Only to be back 20 minutes later with a sprained ankle gasping for a Vodka and Tonic and promising never to do that again. The only New Year's Resolution I have succeeded at was the one that began 'Go Out Less'.

Wishful thinking with an eye on the outcome, but not the journey to the goal is just blinding yourself with fantasy. I want you to do more than wishful thinking.

I want you to follow through on the plan, build your strategy and action it. I want you to succeed but you need to commit and not shy away from taking the alternative path.

Unlike a recent client of the *Dateist*. Let's call her Sheila. She's a 65-year-old, tall blonde who is out and about with a busy social schedule. Monday is choir, Tuesday Tennis, Wednesday 's Bridge, Thursday Book Club and so on. Friday and Saturday she'll go to the movies, concert, or meet friends for dinner. You'd think with such a packed schedule she'd meet someone wouldn't you. Why would she? Think of the logic. It's all very nice ... all very busy and all very …..well girlie. So while of course men play bridge, read books, play tennis etc, Sheila's busy schedule wasn't helping her meet her tman. Put Sheila's diary under the microscope and it's pretty obvious she's waiting for the right man to float toward her raft. She wasn't targeting her search, but she was having a busy time as a single woman. Ok if she wants to stay that way. But my research team made one small suggestion to Sheila to tweak that schedule in a way that would help her meet the man she had outlined in her very precise list of characteristics. So, we gave Sheila's objective some thought, researched, and then planned where she was likely to find a high concentration of the men she was looking for in her home town. But was she prepared to do even the simplest of things? No. Sheila's response was to reject the suggestion on the basis that she didn't have an interest in the subject present in the location we were sending her to, despite our repeatedly telling her that it didn't matter. What was important was her kind of man would be in that location on specific dates at specific times. And in abundance. Go we said. But it was too far out of Sheila's comfort zone. We made a suggestion and all Sheila needed to do was give it a go. All she had to do was TURN UP. That's as difficult as it would get.

Sheila is probably still snug in her busy schedule right now wondering if George Clooney is ever going to walk her way looking for cosy slippers for the fireside. But, hey at least she's still enjoying her game of Bridge

Have you written your list of specifications? The absolute must haves you want in a man before you'll even consider someone. That impossible list.

What you are most likely to have done is the following. Because this is what all women mistakenly do.

1. Join a few dating sites.
2. Sign up with an introductory agency
3. Increase your hobbies and activities
4. Tell your friends

5. Join a club and sit at the bar.
6. Go out with your female friends wearing something risky.

**Outcome**

**The dating sites:-**

These have any number of liars, scroungers, sharksters, drunks, misfits, weirdos – and in there somewhere will be some nice guys. Good luck with finding them. Queuing up at the post office to send yet another disappointing parcel back to Amazon will seem like a doddle after your 100th disappointing date with a weirdo.

To help you navigate the nightmare of dating sites I've written a chapter full of helpful handy hints. Oooh, it sounds like a housekeeping manual.

**The introduction agency: -**

Usually this is expensive. You'll be paying over the odds for somebody that could be .......odd? The agency price could be anywhere between £5-20k. You are paying through the nose, for who knows what kind of nose. Could be a small nose, a snub nose, a huge honker of a nose. Sorry did you forget to specify nose? Or height, colour of hair, teeth, cleanliness, humour? You are paying for goods you haven't seen, and your specifications are open for interpretation. Is the cost worth it? I have a negative view of these agencies because I meet the men and women who have tried this route and have been disappointed. It does work sometimes but my advice is don't be blinded by the promise. Read the contract carefully. What exactly are the agency legally obliged to do for you?

## Increase your hobbies and activities: -

Unless you're planning to reach your dotage being able to sing, dance the samba and play a mean game of bridge… don't bother. Yes, it's a great idea to find a new hobby but think outside the box about the hobby you choose. Otherwise you will find your new hobby is crowded with women just like you.

## Tell your friends: -

Oh yeah ….. like the sisterhood is really going to want to see you snogging George Clooney. Get real. Chances are you'll find yourself sitting opposite a man on a blind date – a bloke your friend said was 'made for you' wondering who exactly your friend thinks you are? And if George Clooney is in her address book, then believe me, she's saving that one for herself. When it comes to men it's every sister for herself. And if she's got any sugar daddies in her contact book, he'll be short on sugar and heavy on the old daddy. I heard a phrase the other day …. 'Purse not Nurse'. I haven't taken my fingers out of my ears yet at that one.

## Join a club:-

And why not? Go sit at the bar with all the other desperately single women.

## Go out with your female friends:-

Don't be ridiculous. Men will run a mile.

## Tip

If you want to meet a man you've got to be prepared to play in his playground.

Now to that list of specifications you've written up. Of course, you've written one – even if it's in your head. He must be X. He must be Y. He must be Z. I can guess what's on it because I've seen and heard it many times before. If that person you are looking for exists, he's one in a million.

So you need to chuck the specifications and drill down to what really matters.

That's what I did when I was thinking of selling my house and moving. My problem was I didn't know where I wanted to move to. Lots of places to go ..... too many on the list. Too many specifics. Too many 'I wants'. It was all too confusing. It was unlikely that I would find everything that was on my list, so which was the most important. The town or the country? Which part of the country? By the sea? In Fenland? In the Dales? On the outskirts of London? Move to a cathedral city or a university town? My head was spinning then a friend gave me some good advice. To stop being specific and analyse exactly how I wanted to spend each hour of the day. So I wrote a timetable. It specified what I wanted to do at each hour of the day. What to do at 8am. What do I do at 9 then at 10 and so on and so on. By that means I discovered that I wanted to walk the dog in the country, take my laptop and have a coffee in a busy high street, get into London quickly, come home and work, go back into London in the evening. There aren't many places you can do that so asking those specific questions meant that I was able to narrow down the locations that could offer what I was looking for. I threw out the list of fantasy specifications and now live happily in the South East of England because it has all those hourly specifics.

So what my friend helped me do is drill down. Now you need to drill down.

I am going to show you how to do the same with your list of specifications. What are you really, really looking for in a man? What really matters? When you have a very clear profile then you'll be able to work out where that person is. How they spend their time. You'll know when your profiled man takes the train. If he works all day, then when do you think he goes food shopping? He doesn't prioritise it in his working day. The healthy fit man does though. What sports does he do? Who are his friends? Decide what matters to you and use it to guide you in your search. Who is the man for you and what does he do – and therefore where is he likely to be. More of that in a later chapter but be prepared to throw it all out the window. Love isn't that prescriptive.

Of course, luck may play its cards and the right man could swim up to your raft, walk into your bridge club. It's happened. Way before time began a girl was stretched out on the grass enjoying the lunchtime sun in Grosvenor Square Gardens. A tall handsome blonde man asked her the time. They are still together 40 years later. It happens. But when you are 45+ it happens less. What we need to do is stretch you out in the sun wherever your ideal man hangs out. Less chance, more increased opportunity.

Here's a wonderful love story for you. It's one of my favourites. It happened long ago, just after the second world war in 1947.

## Pamela. 89

I remember it was a very cold night. One of those evenings when you can see your breath and although my coat was wool it was too thin. I was standing outside the locked, wrought iron gates of the College of Agriculture in Essex. Just one small lantern illuminated the growing darkness. I was cold and I was nervous. I remember I was wearing my best pale blue frock and I kept smoothing down the folds. I really wanted to look my best. I was going on a date with the best-looking boy at the college. He was the dreamboat of the day. Handsome, rugby-playing Dan was cocky and a bit too full of his own self-importance, but I was impressed and flattered that I was the focus of his attention. He came from a rich Norfolk farming family, and I was the precious, but hard-working only child of a Derbyshire farming couple. Our farm was tiny, but I wanted to work it, so here I was miles from home for the first time in my life learning new farming techniques so that I could be useful at home. Looking back, I realise how shy I was - and innocent. I was just 18 and the only reason I'd been allowed to go was because I had an aunt in a nearby village with whom

I could stay. I had told her that I was going to a college event that evening. If I'd told her I was meeting a boy she would not have allowed it, but I had promised to be back no later than 10. Dan had just sauntered over to me in a college coffee break. I remember flushing red as he got closer. I really was that shy and when he asked me to go with him to the dance on Friday, I could barely stammer a yes. He wouldn't have taken no as an answer anyway. He was the kind of boy who got what he wanted. At the time I felt honoured, overwhelmed at being asked. Other girls in the common room were staring with what I assume must have been envy, or possibly disbelief. I was so excited. Thrilled. A date with a boy to go to a dance. And not just anybody but Dan Hayford-Harris. When I think about it now, what was I doing? If he'd respected me at all he would have collected me from my aunts but instead he told me he'd meet me at 7pm outside the college gates. And so there I was. Waiting sharply at 7pm - nervous, shy, and cold. Ten minutes later I was even colder and actually a bit scared. It was quiet and I was alone, but I waited.

## Alec 89

I was in the pub that night. Dan was my roommate - but that was all. I can't say I liked him. Arrogant arse that he was. I knew he was meant to be meeting a girl that night because he'd been boasting about it all week and betting with his mates how far he could get with her. I didn't know who the girl was, but I felt pretty sorry for her. At the time I saw Dan he was drunk, obnoxious, and flirting with one of the barmaids. He'd forgotten about the girl and the dance. Forgotten or didn't care.

I thought about how awful it would be for her to be waiting for someone who didn't turn up. I didn't know who she was, but I did think she would probably be quite frightened, standing on her own in the cold waiting for someone who was never going to show up. Even if Dan did get there it wouldn't be much fun. Drunk and unpleasant as he was. So, I thought I'd go find her. No one deserves to be stood up by an inconsiderate idiot like Dan. So I left the pub, got on my bike, and peddled the two miles to the gates of the College

It was 7.20 when I got there. I didn't know the girl but there was this sweet pretty girl shivering with cold standing alone. I didn't want her to feel foolish or embarrassed, so I lied about Dan and said that he'd been feeling unwell and gone home. So could I take her to the dance instead? I was warmish from my fast bike ride, so I gave her my scarf and coat to drape over her shoulders. I was really worried as she was shaking with the chill, so we walked rapidly to the dance and I took her in. I think it was in the light of the ticket hall that I first really looked at her and realised just how pretty she was. Shiny brown curly hair, beautiful blue eyes with long black lashes and a shy smile. I think I fell in love right there and then, and 70 years later I look at her and still feel the same.

## Pamela

Even when it got to 7.15, I still thought Dan would come. I remember that the thick East Anglian fog had descended, and my aunt's house was some way from the college, I didn't have a torch and the gates behind me were locked and there was no one around. I was worried and I did start to get a sneaking suspicion that I might have been stood up but surely Dan couldn't be so awful? Then in the distance I saw a small bike light getting bigger and breathed a sigh of relief. Dan. At last. On a bike.

Was I disappointed? Initially yes. But I thought what a good friend and a decent man Alec must be to come all this way and let me know Dan couldn't make it. It wasn't until later in the evening when Dan turned up at the dance drunk and with the barmaid from the Red Lion that I knew the truth. Drunk Dan was rather revolting. Alec on the other hand was funny, kind, well mannered, barely drank and danced beautifully. Three years after College we got married and went back to Derbyshire to help run my parents' farm. With Alec's inheritance we bought up more land. We've brought up our sons here and one of whom now works the farm. I couldn't have had a happier life. I'm very lucky to have met Alec. He has been my rock. From that day onwards when he first made that kind gesture, he has shown me over and over again what a wonderful, thoughtful man he is. Lucky me that I definitely got the better man.

## Chapter Two

## LET'S START WITH HAPPINESS.

*There is love, of course, and then there's life, its enemy. Jean* Anouilh

But then there's laughter - like a lick from a puppy it cures all.

Laughter is the essential ingredient of love. The saviour of the day. There is no love without laughter and no laughter without love. Laughter is a barometer of happiness. And happiness is attractive.

You need to be happy in yourself before you go looking for love.

Strange that! Misery is unattractive. Who would have thought it!

If you're happy then you are ready to meet someone. If you're not happy then what on earth are you selling? Because what man is buying misery? Is anyone buying misery?

We've all got enough of our own troubles and finding someone to share those troubles with is all too often playing a role in the desire for a relationship. A real friendship is one where problems are shared but that, if shared at all, can really only come way down the line of any friendship. Putting your troubles in the shop window is not very inviting. It's the equivalent of meeting a doctor at a drinks party and asking if he'll take a look at your bunion. Sharing your troubles up front doesn't oil the wheels to a new relationship - it stops it bang in its tracks.

Happiness and success in love can only begin with happiness in yourself.

So what is happiness? Well now there's a complex question. Certainly, it's not the same for everybody. How boring would that be? But one thing is for sure if you are not happy in yourself then you are not really ready for a relationship. You cannot expect that a relationship will make you completely happy. Never put that much expectation or pressure on a man.

Man is not a life support system. Gin is.

Only you know what makes you happy and only you can make you truly happy. (If happiness is any kind of a complete achievable goal anyway. We all put too much expectation on a 'right' to happiness). And that expectation is not helped by social media either, where everyone seems happy. If you're having a bad day, then don't go looking on Facebook etc at everyone else's life. No one ever posts that they've had a miserable day, scoffed three Big Mac's and several tubs of ice cream. It's always people beaming with delight at a great restaurant, party etc or yoga posing in a tight leotard.

A relationship will not suddenly make you happy. Ask yourself when you have been happiest. I hope it's when you have been at your busiest and you had a boyfriend/partner/husband to share things with some of the time. A man can bring additional happiness to your life but it's unfair to expect him to be the source of your entire happiness and the complete focus of your life. If that's your expectation then you are not only adding unnecessary pressure to a relationship, but you are setting yourself up for a very high fall. If the relationship ends, then you may well find yourself feeling like you have nothing. Having a life that is full and enjoyable with or without a man is healthy. This means that if it looks like your relationship is on the rocks – not only do you have a life to support you, but you are not vulnerable to being taken advantage of by a man who thinks you are dependent on him, and solely on him, for your happiness.

We can all create or find moments where there is happiness. For some people it's writing a new song, baking a cake, coming across a beautiful view, or a simple lunch with friends. Happiness can be found in the warm evening sunshine, the beauty of nature, the peace of a church pew, the bluebells appearing in the woods, the attractive window cleaner or watching your neighbour reverse into a lamppost.

But whatever happiness is, it definitely is not something we should expect to source from one person.

*Delissa Needham*

There's also happiness in helping others. In the words of Prince Philip – if you think it's all about you then you will never be happy.

Ex partners can often be a bucket load of misery. Don't bring them into your new relationship by mentioning who they are, talking about that experience, or even referring to the ex. No matter what you say about the ex you are unlikely to look good in the story. If you ended the relationship, then you'll look unfeeling – if he ended it then you'll look unwanted. So take that truck load of ex-partner misery and drive it off the edge of a cliff. By all means learn from the experience but don't haul it around by bringing the ex's out of the cupboard and into your new relationship. Tomorrow is a new day and a new world – forget what went wrong with your previous partners, or husband. There is a time to share those war stories but it's not 'til you are way down the line and only then if you really think it adds something. Be light and funny and save the serious stuff for much later. Don't shovel any of your dirt in the direction of the new man in your life. Apart from anything else it's boring. So pull yourself together and get on with the tomorrow of your love. Chuck out the bad stuff. I recently watched a small boy called Sid, sitting cross-legged in front of his toy box going through it and throwing over his shoulder what he didn't need. He was making superfast decisions about a toy train, a carriage, a small spade, a model car etc. It all went rapidly over his shoulder until all he was left with was his trucks. Sid could soon sort out the rubbish stored in the attic or that useless drawer in the kitchen, or the junk in the garden shed. I think we could all do with a version of Sid in our heads - chucking out the bad stuff like ex-partner troubles, and just keeping the 'trucks' of life that genuinely bring you joy.

Laughter is an essential part of your opening conversation when meeting a new man. That first banter and first flirt has got to be different, stand out and if possible, funny. Asking someone where they come from, what they do and where they live are the most boring conversation starters of all time. Some of the advice that other coaches give women on what to say when chatting up a man are so cliche that I cringe when reading them. Men like women who are decisive, confident, self-assured, and feminine with it. That's a wonderful mixed bag of desirability that takes a lot of talent to pull off, but it needs to become second nature to you.

Be confident, be self-assured but be feminine – and show that you love to laugh, that you are happy and that you really do enjoy amusing fun conversation. It's not that hard if you listen, respond, and think.

When it comes to chat up lines, here's a good one. A friend had a part-time job behind the bagel counter of a bakery in London's east end. It was a favourite hangout for anyone leaving a club in the early hours. The bakery was open all night. Gemma was behind the counter when this guy came in with his friends. It was only her first day on the job, but it was fun …everyone who came in through the door late at night was in a party mood. Greg was not.

28

He was a doctor finishing a very late-night shift at the nearby hospital and on his way home from work. He could do with a bagel and Gemma thought he could with a laugh so when he asked for a bagel, she asked him if he wanted the hole extra-large. He smiled for the first time all night and he came back the next night of course and so on 'til he asked her out and that was that. They've been laughing ever since.

Laughter is a great ice breaker and when women laugh it's invariably sexy and engaging, although historically speaking the female journey hasn't exactly been much to laugh at. We only got the right to vote in 1928 and it's been a slow uphill struggle since then. Only just the other day my colleague was wondering why it is that in 2022 women are in a diversity category! It feels like society is not set up for women to succeed. What's really changed things for us has been the onset of technology. It's altered the workforce so it's more office based and less physical. More mental power and less physical prowess. As a result, the female workforce has grown and with it, independence. The traditional roles of the wife being 'stay at home' and men being the money earners has changed.

And of course this has impacted on the relationship between men and women.

Equality is justly a right for us all but there have been casualties along the way. Women seem to shy away from being feminine now. As though it's a sign of weakness when it should be seen as one of the balls in a brilliant juggling act. An extra tool in our tool kit. Why can't we be strong, focussed, determined and yet still be all the delightful softness that is being a woman. It's not betraying your sex to be charming to a man. You can be true to who you are and what you want in life, AND at the same time be all the delightful characteristics of a woman. Women have a natural ability to be gentle, compassionate, to care and to be an understanding friend etc. But all too often the ideal relationship that women seek with a man is viewed as some sort of 'consorting with the enemy'. It is not. And you will not happily have a relationship with a man if you view it as such. It's not a battle of women v men. No wonder men feel confused. Men aren't encouraged to be men anymore and women don't want to be feminine or flirty. Oh dear it's all such a shambles. Where's the fuel for the bedroom? If you make a man feel less of a man out of the bedroom, he won't be much of a man in it. And unfortunately for men the older they get the more they have the added worry about what the heart wants that the body can't achieve.

Well I have the perfect answer. Yes, I do. The solution that will make men feel like men and women feel like women again. It's all in a jar of pickles.

Ask your man to open a jar you've been seemingly struggling with, praise him even when he looks like he's going to have a heart attack over it and when he finally succeeds in his labours be as delighted as if he'd just rescued a drowning puppy. You'll be surprised how proud and happy he will be. It will serve you well.

*Delissa Needham*

Do not point out that you could have done it by simply running it under the hot tap or piercing the lid.

## Charlotte 87

I was sort of 'on the run'. Getting away from a bad relationship and a broken heart. I was definitely NOT looking for love. I was going to South Africa to stay with my cousin and travelling there by sea. I had boarded the boat in Southampton heading for Cape Town. Two days into the journey I went on deck after dinner. It was a moonlight night, and the sea was relatively calm. Not surprisingly someone else was also on deck. Leaning over the railing and looking down at the water was a man in a dinner jacket smoking a cigarette. In the background I could hear the music from the jazz band coming up the stairwell. It was the sound of the 1930's - a long forgotten song by Jack Buchanan "I'll go my way by myself". It couldn't have been more appropriate for how I felt. The man turned and smiled at me. Looking back I suppose you could say it was a perfect romantic meeting. But it wasn't. The last thing I ever wanted EVER again was another relationship. At that moment I thought all men were absolute cads.

## James 88

I went onto the deck after dinner to enjoy a cigarette. It was a beautiful evening, and I could hear the band in the distance. I should've been on the dance floor, but I really didn't want to be around people much at that time. It would've been quicker to fly but I hate flying since I lost both my parents in a plane crash - hence I had chosen to travel by sea. I was going to Cape Town to take up a new job as an engineer. It was an exciting opportunity for me but mainly I just wanted to get as far away from London and England as I could. My girlfriend, my fiancé, had decided to leave me for my best friend so I had suffered the ultimate double whammy. Since we all shared the same circle of friends, to have stayed in London would have been unbearable. I remember looking out to sea and feeling sorry for myself then I realised someone else was on deck. When I looked to my right, I saw a girl standing there looking like she wasn't sure whether to go back down below or stay where she was. I remember I offered her a cigarette and made some lame comment about the moonlight.

## **Charlotte**

He looked like such a sad and lonely figure. Something about him seemed so lost and I felt my presence on the deck was almost an intrusion. I wasn't sure if I should just go back down below or go to the rail on the other side but then he offered me a cigarette. I remember we had a nice conversation. Very relaxed and he had this lovely soft voice and kind eyes. He was quite formal at first but then he became more relaxed. When I said good night to him and left the deck to go to my cabin, I rather hoped that I'd bump into him again very soon. It was five days to Cape Town and over that time I found myself enjoying his company more and more. We had dinner together two nights later. He was amusing company and so interesting. When we arrived in Cape Town he asked if we could meet up

*Delissa Needham*

again soon. I said yes of course and gave him my cousin's address, but then it all went terribly wrong. There was a message waiting for me at my cousin's. My father had died suddenly of a heart attack while I was on board ship and so I was on the next flight out. I did come back to Cape Town but not until a year later and I never expected to see James again - or if I did, I expected him to be married or whatever. But I was pleasantly surprised when I ran into him at a private party a month or so after I arrived back. Truth be told I had been looking out for him, but Cape Town is a big place. It was definitely fate playing a hand. We went out to dinner and started seeing each other properly and then on New Year's Eve, almost a year and a half after we first met, he proposed. I said yes straightaway and so we've built our lives and family while living here in Cape Town. Three children and five grandchildren later, I often think how lucky I was to be on board that ship at that particular time. But I do wonder about things. The 'what ifs'. Supposing it hadn't been a full moon that night. Would I have gone up on deck? Probably not? If the sea had been rough instead of calm or if James hadn't fancied a cigarette at that particular moment. Whatever. I'm just glad it all swung into place and as a consequence I've had a                                     very happy life.

*Chapter Three*

# DO YOU NEED HELP WITH YOUR SELF CONFIDENCE?

Are you Queen Boudica or a shrinking violet? So you would like someone to share things with. You've decided it's time for a new man, for a new romance. You will no doubt have your own personal circumstances that have brought you to this point. There are numerous reasons why we women find ourselves looking for a new relationship and it can feel scary. It takes confidence and huge belief in a positive outcome for any of us to go on this journey. You probably know from experience that it's not easy because the road ahead is paved with many pitfalls and disappointments. You will need inner strength, a lot of self-belief and a great deal of confidence. If you're at this point because of a break-up in a relationship, then your confidence is probably dented. When there's a break-up no one really escapes unharmed. So, acknowledge to yourself that you may well be feeling a little bruised.

If you are at this point because you are now widowed, then you have probably been in a safe and cosy situation for some time. You probably never expected to be in this situation. You had expected to go on into your later life with that one person and friend by your side. For that and many other reasons the thought of dating someone again must be so difficult to even think about. You still love that person you have lost but they are no longer physically present. That person is not replaceable, you don't want to replace them, so you are not even sure you want to try, and yet you feel so alone. Try to think of it differently. Try to think that you are not looking to replace them, instead you are looking for someone with whom you will now move into a new phase of your life. You are not replacing anyone. Just stepping forward in life. Deciding you want to do that is your first step. You are not the only one in your position. The feelings are unique to you. The situation is not. How many lonely people just like you do you think there are?? It doesn't matter what age you are – 35, 45, 55, 65, 75 - whatever. There are people for whatever reason who feel lonely and would like to meet someone, and not necessarily for a relationship. Or sex. Maybe you just want to meet someone to go to the cinema with and talk about the film afterwards. Someone of the opposite sex to have lunch with. A friend who isn't a female friend. Someone to give you a hug and share laughter and life's adventure with. That doesn't need to be someone who moves into your life and your home. There are people who, like you, want someone of the opposite sex to spend time with.

I also wonder if you are one of the people reading this book because you feel you have already given the idea of meeting someone your best shot. You tried and didn't succeed, and you didn't enjoy the trying so now you've given up.

Whatever your reason for bravely taking steps to start a new relationship it is likely your confidence needs a boost. What can you do that will 're-confidence' you? What small tasks can be achieved that are relatively easy but will make you feel good about yourself. And when you do achieve something, write it down. If someone pays you a compliment, then write it down. That way you can remind yourself. It's all too easy to forget the positive and lovely things that happen to us when we are focussed on the negative (such as the end of a relationship). Get yourself a small notebook – your 'Re-confidence Me' book – and write down the nice things that happen. Then open it and read it when you fancy a boost.

If you seriously want to increase your chances of meeting someone then you've got to be gutsy. A no confidence state of mind is a non-starter. You will need confidence to succeed in this journey. There is a time and a place to be reserved but this situation is not it. You can't be a shrinking violet. You need the confidence to say hello to strangers. To strike up conversations with anyone – because anyone may lead to someone. And because the landscape is crowded with competition you need to be confident enough to seize every opportunity to introduce yourself to strangers. Don't say I can't. Say I can and I will.

So, how stiff is the competition? Well the statistics paint an interesting picture.

Men are more likely to remarry, with 64% of men and 52% of women having remarried. Women over the age of 55, however, are far less likely to get remarried, due to many reasons but one being that many (54%) just do not want to.

So if you are over 55 and reading this book, I assume you are in the 45% who do. That means that in your age group for every ten single women, just a little more than 4 are seriously really wanting to meet someone. You are so serious you envisage yourself re-married. That puts you ahead of the other women who may say they're interested and willing to go along with plans to meet someone, but you are the more likely to find someone because you really, really want to. You're prepared to do what it takes to achieve your goal. Aren't you?

However, when single people say they can't be bothered and they've given up looking, the hope is still there. Of course it is. The human condition is such that we are all looking to love and be loved. Being alone is unhealthy – mentally and physically. The difference between you and the 54% of wishful thinkers is that yours is more than whimsy. You have determination. You must also have courage. You have to be able to turn to an unknown man at a party and ask, "haven't we met before?". Somebody said that to me once and I smartly quipped back – yes it was a wife swapping party in 1993. Witty yes but I was in a job interview at the time, so not so clever hey? I know it's difficult to say hello to people you don't know but what's the worst that can happen? Fear of looking stupid or being rejected? To someone you have just met? Really? This is where re-confidencing comes into play. It's so important to believe in yourself and remember that everyone, including you, has attractive qualities. Believe in that, even if they are not the qualities that the person you are talking to is looking for. Talk to people. Keep practising. Don't give up. You must get beyond the fear, or you really will find it difficult to meet someone.

Unfortunately dating has a catch 22 about it. You need to date a lot of men to find Mr Right – kiss a lot of frogs etc. And you need confidence for dating, but confidence is constantly the casualty at the end of relationships. If you are that someone who is still feeling bruised from your last relationship, if you're carrying enough baggage to fill a train carriage, then it's a good idea to find a therapist to talk to. Get the inner cupboard tidied up before you start dating. I'll provide you with tips, advice, and strategy on how to find someone and to give you the encouragement to go out and look, but if there's work to be done deep down inside then you need to get on with it. You can boost your confidence on a surface level with a new hairdo, new clothes, a beauty treatment etc. There's nothing like a make-over to make you feel better. But you also need to take your emotional temperature. You cannot go looking for a new relationship if you are still feeling the impact of the last one.

Recent relationships that haven't gone well really can knock you for six. It can be hard and more so when the reason is as basic as someone just doesn't feel the same emotion as you do. Unrequited love is a sad state of affairs. If only it were possible to accept that it's just wonderful to love someone and it doesn't matter if they don't love you back. That surely is true love. To love someone and just want them to be happy. But that's not an easily achievable state of being. Most of us love someone and don't want the unrequited version. We want to be loved back.

It's a horrible feeling when a relationship with someone you thought special crashes down. It's happened to all of us. The path to true love does not run smooth and we know that's no help, but you've got to expect that looking for love isn't easy. Try to learn from the experience and not to let it put you off. There will be plenty of these types of peaks and troughs on your dating journey. You may well find yourself going out with someone a few times and then suddenly they stop calling. You thought you were having a nice time, enjoying each other's company. There was lots of laughter, it was a bit sexy, a bit flirty and then….. suddenly nothing. No follow up date, no other arrangement and for no apparent reason the new relationship has already hit the buffers. It happens. It's disappointing. But it's not unusual. What's important is that you don't let it knock you. Don't over analyse it and try not to let it put you off looking. It's normal to end up analysing what happened and questioning ourselves. Is it because of X or was it because I did Y etc? But all that re-examining your behaviour, calling yourself to account will get you nowhere. If you let self-doubt creep in, you'll end up down a rabbit hole labelled 'what's wrong with me'? Nothing.

For whatever reason – and it will be his reason not yours – he just didn't want to move it up.

My advice is don't invest too early and slow it down. You're not a kid in the playground who picked someone to be your friend then fell out five minutes later over the swing. Real relationships take time. I've seen relationships go from 0 to 60 in three nanoseconds: meet for coffee; meet for dinner; spend every moment together and then… gone in 60 seconds. If it's right, then take the time. Keep your balance and do keep spending time in your usual way with family and friends. If it's right he will still be there. And you will still be standing. Not dazed and confused at what just happened.

Having said that there are a few behaviours to avoid that could well end a relationship. When you are on a date with a man it is because he fancies you so really all you have to do is keep stoking that flame. Sadly though so many women put out the fire without even realising it. So did you genuinely feel there was a chemistry between you both – or was it just something you were feeling because you talked a lot and he listened? Did you bang on for hours about your politics or general views or even worse your problems? Did you engage in a conversational exchange of views and opinions – or did you forget to listen and instead dominated the chat? Did you remember that conversation is a two-way street – you listen then respond. Did you show interest and be interested? Did you flatten all his dreams with your negative responses or were you keen to know what makes his business work, what his dreams are, what drives him or how he enjoys life? Did you find subjects in common that you are both passionate about? Conversation is the foundation of a developing friendship. Is this something you need to work on?

If on the other hand you had a good conversation and you feel strongly that you both enjoyed each other's company then you are probably analysing to an unhealthy degree on why the relationship ended. All those negative reasons you are coming up with for why he never called again though, you really must shake those right out of your head. You don't know and you will never know so don't waste the time stressing over it. Move on. Otherwise, you will be running reasons around your head in the waking hours that have no foundation in reality, like... do you really think he didn't call you back because you're carrying a little extra weight around your tummy? Why did he ask you out in the first place if he didn't like curvy women so forget dragging yourself over the coals for that chocolate biscuit you ate yesterday? Men do of course fantasise about the latest fashion model, actress etc but the world isn't made up of glamorous plastic looking perfect people. Happy relationships are made up of real people and a little extra weight will not get in the way of you being funny, sexy, and great company.

Are you worrying he didn't call you back because he suddenly decided he didn't fancy you? Again why did he take you out in the first place? He found you attractive but maybe the chemistry just didn't click after all, but you didn't just suddenly get ugly overnight. Unless you decided to drop the feminine sexy look he bought into and swap it for combats and army boots. If you went from being fragrant Mary to Miss Aggressive overnight, then that would do it. I admit it's a generalisation, but older men are looking for the feminine woman. French women are particularly good at pulling off the feminine but strong type. Scarily so, but they have the knack for being feminine and sexy while also being strong. Being needy is not sexy to most men. Confidence is. Neither is being overconfident and bullish but being a weak pushover won't get you anywhere, other than with a man who thinks he can treat you like a doormat.

So what else can you do to work on your confidence? If you feel you look your best and you are getting help with any issues, then you may have to start practising talking to strangers. If you are standing in a queue, then strike up a conversation. Say more than just your order to the waiter in a café. Talk to the checkout assistant in your supermarket. Join clubs not with the intention of meeting a man but with the intention of meeting people. Don't spend evenings alone in front of the TV. Get out and do things. The more you do, the more people you meet, the more places you go, the more you achieve for you, the more you will grow in yourself.

How strong is your confidence where sex is concerned? It's a major part of any new relationship but don't forget that men also feel unsure about sex in a new relationship. Especially older men. Lacking confidence or self-assurance around sex as you get older is not a prerogative of one gender over the other. It can be fearful for both of you. Fear of failure can stop a man from wanting to follow through on a relationship. When a relationship ends suddenly it's natural to wonder how much sex played a part. Either to end it or fuel it in the first place. In some cases it was all it was about. There are more men than women dating in older age groups certainly, and some of those men are not looking for a relationship but just sex. It's your task to spot the difference between the ones who just want sex and the ones who are looking for a new partner in life. The men who only want sex don't want commitment, so no matter how good the sex is they won't follow through because that would be taking a step towards a relationship - much easier to go and find another woman. Don't get caught up in that scenario because it's a situation very likely to knock your confidence. Unless a 'just sex' situation is what you want. Otherwise be clear about wanting a relationship and make sure the man you meet feels the same way.

## **TIP:**

The Retread. There must have been men in your past a long way back. Are any of them worth a retread? Are any of them back on the 'market'? Go and dig around in your past. Do a bit of research in your social media. Someone you may have known or fancied or who fancied you may still be holding a candle for you, fanning the flame of a long-held desire. It could be someone you knew 20, 30 or even 40 years ago. Perhaps the timing wasn't right then but now…it just might be…

*How I Met My Man and How You Can Meet Yours*

## Tessa 62

I had been divorced from my husband Roger for nearly 5 years and I knew I wanted to meet someone sooner rather than later. I had this panic that time was running out. It wasn't, but I just wanted to meet someone. So I joined an online dating site. I hated it. Some ok dates but lots of disappointing ones. It all just seemed to reinforce those things that I don't want in my life. Some of the dates were dates from hell. Alcoholics, depressives and one arrogant man who really thought I would have sex with him straightaway. Then one day I was looking through my Facebook and started searching for a few old names from the past. I did the same thing on LinkedIn. Actually I was looking for one person in particular. Julian. We'd gone out together very briefly when I was 19 and we'd had a fun summer together. I think he was quite keen on me but then I met someone else, and Julian went off to take up a job in New York. In 30 years we'd only met each other again once. Quite by accident I saw him in a bar in New York about 15 years ago. We had a drink together and caught up on our news. By now we were in our 40's and both of us were married with children but clearly we still enjoyed each other's company. I knew his wife and children were away but nevertheless I was surprised when he phoned next day to see if I was free for dinner. We did have a great time and I was sorry when we parted company. There was a moment when I thought he was going to kiss me goodbye on the lips, but whatever, there couldn't be anything more. I flew home next and never heard from Julian again. Fifteen years later I came across him on Facebook. After he accepted my friend request, he took to ringing me regularly. About once a week at first - just to chat. And this 'just for a chat' scenario increased to every other day and went on for three years until he announced one day that he was getting divorced. I had got divorced ten years earlier and I knew how it felt. You may think you are ok, but you are not. It doesn't matter who is leaving who, it is still a time of grief for a lost relationship. Nevertheless I needed to keep my distance from Julian. I didn't want to be the catalyst for his marriage break up so to make sure it stayed purely platonic, we never met. We only spoke on the phone. Julian eventually got divorced. The breakup of the marriage was not about any third party but about two people who had simply grown apart. Then for the first time in nearly two decades we did eventually meet. We finally moved in together and we've been together ever since. We rekindled a love that had first begun some 40 years earlier. For me it goes to show that what happened in the past may not necessarily stay in the past.

*Chapter Four*

# WHAT'S TROUBLING YOU? WHY SORTING YOUR MIND IS SUCH AN IMPORTANT FIRST STEP.

This is all part of the business of being ready. If you are not ready you won't be successful at meeting someone new.

If you are single, and it's been your status for some time then most likely you are used to it. It's great that you are proactively doing something to change that. But if you are someone recently divorced, or widowed, or have just experienced a bad breakup, then shaking yourself down and starting again is tough. And that's partly because along with accepting your new situation you also have to cope with the physical impact of being suddenly alone. Don't underestimate how it will affect you.

Primarily your body will notice the absence of Oxytocin. This is a hormone involved in childbirth and breast-feeding. But crucially for you it is also associated with relationships. It's called the "love hormone" because it thrives on touch. A hug stimulates oxytocin. It's also an appetite control hormone, so small wonder when that when you are not being nourished by physical affection you reach for the ice cream. The hormones are the result of our carefully balanced endocrine system. So that includes your happy hormones like serotonin, dopamine etc but it all goes a bit wobbly when your relationship crashes to a halt. No wonder the ending of a relationship is a painful experience.

Analysis shows that women have had an average of three breakups by the age of 30 with at least one of them impacting us strongly enough that our quality of life is affected. Researchers from Birmingham University and University College London asked 5705 people in 95 countries to rate their pain after a breakup. They found that women tended to be more negatively affected (6.84) vs men (6.58) in terms of physical pain. Emotional pain rated at 4.21 for women vs 3.75 for men. Breakups do appear to hit women harder. The good news is that women tend to recover more fully and come out emotionally stronger. Men, it appears, never fully recover, they just move on. Men have been heard saying splitting up is like a bad toothache. Pull the tooth and after a while the pain goes away. But if their dog dies …..wow that pain lasts forever.

It staggers me that the number for women is not higher judging by some of the conversations I've had over the years. It's not nice, it's not fair, but it happens. It's what you do about it that's important. Most crucially give yourself some time. So before you slap on the make-up and head out of the door have a think.

There are important things you must do first when you have made the decision to re-join the dating game.

## 1. Responsibility: The Blame Game

Naturally when it's all over, piling on the pain by admitting your share of the breakdown is pretty difficult. It's much easier at this juncture to wholly blame your significant other for the breakdown in a relationship. We all do it. Self-reflection is hard when you are in the pain of a relationship ending. It's easier to blame others than take any responsibility ourselves. But conversely neither are you wholly to blame. Be fair to yourself. It's not all your fault either, no matter what has been said or how you have been made to feel. But accepting some of the blame is the only way you can grow and learn from the experience. Turn something bad into something good.

## 2. Honesty and Change.

We change as human beings, all the time. It`s how great things happen. Change is healthy. If we didn't change, the ability to burp the national anthem at aged 19 would still be funny at 40. People change and develop over time. But those in a long relationship don't always change and develop at the same pace. That's when things can go wrong. But a relationship slipping off the rails can happen for a myriad of reasons. Some of which you have no control over. The key is being able to be honest. Stand back and assess what happened. It wasn't all his fault. Was it? What did you have control over? The answer should be 'me'. Think about how you could have done things differently, but don't beat yourself up about it. It's in the past now but admitting your <u>share</u> of responsibility is one of the healthiest things you can do for your well-being. Knowing and understanding what happened is information that will help you develop so you go into a new relationship better able to meet your needs and that of a partner. Put the past behind you. Learn from the experience. The ending of a relationship for good or bad is a lesson and one that helps you to change and grow. Be grateful. It takes time but one day you will be able to look back on your last relationship from the distance of time. We hope that you will feel grateful for the memories you shared and be glad of what you learnt. The moment you can say thank you is when you are truly free. I hope you will be able to admit your own faults and honestly take your share of the blame, so that you're able to take valuable self-knowledge into a new relationship with someone else.

Accept but don't be a victim.

Stuff happens to all of us, some big things, some small. Accept that bad things happen even to good people. Don't let a bad breakup define who you are. Identifying why it happened is healthy, so that it can be avoided in future, but lingering in the victim role is unhealthy and won't help you grow as a person. It's also not attractive. Remember you don't get around bad situations, you just get through them so let's look at ways to do this:

## 3. Professional help.

If your boiler broke down, you would call a plumber. If your computer goes on the fritz an IT specialist is at hand. But when the mind is disturbed many of us are reluctant or hesitant to seek help. Psychiatry, or counselling, or analysts are often viewed with suspicion. Yet we listen to our friends who are much more likely to be unconsciously or even consciously biased. It's simple, if you want independent support and to talk to someone who knows how to listen, how to move you forward, and will do so with your best interests at heart then go see a professional therapist. Find one you are comfortable with. At the very least they can provide coping mechanisms, both short and long term. They allow you a safe space to express your innermost feelings without judgement. Putting those feelings into words can be the first step towards moving on. Looking at your feelings about events in the cold rational light of day in the therapist's room is going to be a lot more beneficial than trying to do the same with a bottle of wine, which is not the most useful response to a breakup.

## 4. Consider where you seek advice.

Friends are great. The lifeblood of most women. Great girl friendships are the stuff of legend. But when you talk to friends you have to feel sure your feelings will be treated with confidence. You need to feel certain that friends will know what's in your best interests. And sometimes their advice is not impartial. Whether consciously or unconsciously, friends may also be thinking of themselves. Take Miranda. Should her friends have advised her to get divorced?

Miranda was happily married to the most organised man on the planet. The kind that has the dishwasher sorted according to plate size, cutlery type and pan usage. He even rearranged her hair accessory drawer into colour and use. The garden was designed to his specifications. It was very reflective of the affluence of the area, so basically it just looked like everyone else`s. Sooooo dull. Then one day Miranda discovered that her husband was having an affair. How? An estate agent rang to take photos of the house to make up the 'for sale' particulars. It was the first she'd heard of it. It was a bit of a shock to say the least. I would have loved to have heard how that conversation played out.

What was she to do? All her friends advised her to get divorced. They even provided lawyer details and property advice. But to Miranda that was an, all too easy, knee jerk reaction. Why 'throw the baby out with the bathwater'? Miranda was fortunate enough to get some very good impartial and professional advice. She listened. She realised her husband was having an awful time at work and was not in control. Miranda thought he would sort it out like he always did and so she hadn't put in the effort to support him. So someone else did. Talking didn't come easy either to Miranda or her husband. So instead she took action and communicated instead through the garden. She dug up the boring plants from the front of the house, put them in a pile and planted the ones she wanted. On his arrival home he was confronted with piles of earth and a grubby driveway. It started a conversation, which led to another conversation - the one they should have been having all along. Once they had started honestly communicating about what was really affecting them and supporting each other the storm passed, and many years later they are still together. Choosing plants makes them laugh.

Miranda's friends' advice to her was clearly not in her best interests. But Miranda being single would have made other single women feel more comfortable with their own status. Another divorcee to join the club. Another new playmate. Another stool taken in the wine bar of life. Every good friend will listen, but eventually you must and will get over a breakup through your own strength.

When a bad break up happens, spending your days sunk in the wine lake of Europe trying to drown your sorrows will not help you. Nor will overanalyzing it. Don't wallow, do your best to get out into the world, meet people, lots of people and then you may begin to move forward. Let's hope you haven't used all your girlfriend tokens up in the process.

Be honest, take some of the responsibility, some of the blame, grow and learn from the knowledge and remember to go easy and be kind to yourself. If you can, go somewhere where there is no memory of the ex. If only for a few hours. It will help put a distance between you and your sorrows. A weekend break in a new city, a walk in a new wood. Visiting an old friend that you haven't had time for in a while (but don't dump on them, they have their own stuff to deal with). Being alone for the first time in ages is hard. Talking your friends' ears off won't change it, but the distractions of new experiences will eventually help you feel better.

Give it thought and reflect, but when the ice cream bowl is empty and the bottles are at the recycling bank, then it's time to take back control of who you are and what you want. Time to move on.

# PART 2: WHAT YOU NEED TO KNOW

*Chapter Five*

# WHAT MEN WANT AND WHAT WOMEN WANT.

### What is attraction and what do you need to know about it?

We all want someone to love and someone to love us. Or perhaps you just want someone to share your life with, to do things with and to enjoy a special friendship with. Someone to care about, who will care about you. That goal is as old as the day the first caveman donned his best loin cloth and set off in search of the perfect woman. Caveman would drag one back to his dwelling by her hair if he had to. Thankfully we've come a long way since then and having your precious follicles tested for strength isn't compulsory for dating anymore. Theoretically it should be easier for you to find your perfect partner with today's amazing technology. We are now in a world where someone can see your photo, think wow, then swipe right and arrange to meet you. That initial action is fuelled by visual attraction. For men particularly. The best looking gets noticed and that's true whether you're looking for love online or in the real world.

Attraction is the start line. Its basis is both biological and psychological, and often has roots in personal experience. Memory plays a part in attraction. You see something you recognise about a person – it could be deck shoes or a type of walk and you subconsciously associate it with something in your past that pulls strings. What attracts is different for everyone and thankfully people rarely agree on what's attractive and what isn't. But for the purposes of finding love you need to understand what men find attractive. It's very different from what women find attractive.

Let's go back to our caveman. When he was dragging his bride home the chances are she had childbearing hips and a face that suggested good genes. If she'd consented to be dragged to a new dwelling, then she'd probably have taken one look at Zog and decided he was up to the job of putting food on the table. In that sense we haven't changed much. The two genders are responding instinctively to very different but very basic biological requirements for the survival of the human race. Ask women what they find attractive in a man and it's more about qualities that are attached to strength – intelligence, success, power, financial stability. Men on the other hand are looking for the mother of their children so for them attraction is very visual i.e blonde v brunette, big or small breasts etc, etc.

There is a series of documentaries made for television which set out to examine the differences between men and women,

*Delissa Needham*

and particularly to look at what men find attractive. The documentaries were built around a number of interesting visual experiments to determine how differently the genders behave around the opposite sex. One of those experiments set out to either prove or disprove some recently published new research in the Lancet that showed men are more visually aroused than women. Basically it said that men have sex glands in their eyes. So the team set out to test this theory. What happened in a real-life experiment was fascinating. I was the Executive Producer of the documentaries, and I was astounded at what the experiment revealed about men and attraction. Cameras were set up on a balcony overlooking Liverpool Street railway station. The production team had hired an attractive model with long legs, and lovely long blonde hair to leave the train as it arrived in the station and walk out across the concourse to a taxi. She was visually striking, and she was struggling to carry a very heavy suitcase. As she left the train she was spotted by a group of men. One of them stepped forward and offered to carry the case. He was the most attractive of the group and clearly viewed by the others as the alpha male. All the other guys gathered behind him watching and admiring his progress. Our watching psychologist told us that the peer group leader is silently nominated by the rest of the group as the person most likely to succeed. He carried her case to the taxi all the while leaning towards her, chatting to her and eventually he asked her out. So far so straightforward. We then gave the same suitcase to a brunette. She was a woman of average height and brown hair with nothing at all particular to make her stand out in a crowd.

And she didn't. She carried the heavy suitcase on her own, all the way to the taxi rank. She struggled with difficulty through the crowded concourse and yet she was unnoticed. I know we could have repeated that experiment again and again with the same result. I had run a similar experiment for another tv show five years earlier. On that occasion we filmed an attractive brunette walking through a crowded street – then we put the same girl in a blonde wig and filmed the 'head turning' difference. Blondes really do have more fun.

The point of telling you about these experiments is to make you aware that you need to be noticed. You don't have to be blonde to achieve that, but you can't dress to melt into the background in a crowded landscape.

Psychological studies tell us that blondes are seen as more approachable. Be that as it may – blondes do lead the field in the attraction stakes. Is this just because they are visually brighter? And yet there are plenty of brunette women throughout history who are considered beautiful and whom men adore from Sophia Loren to Sandra Bullock. Whatever the colour of your hair the most important thing to remember is that you need to be noticed. If you really want to meet the love of your life, then you need to give yourself the chance of attracting someone. So before you go looking for a partner, understand what attracts and how important it is. Don't undervalue the importance of visual appeal to a potential partner. Couples often meet through a moment of chance – but it's fuelled by attraction. What defines attraction varies from person to person, but you can bet that few people are attracted to unwashed hair, fuzzy legs or sloppy tracky bottoms. Wear what makes you feel good, whether it's lipstick, high heels and pretty dress, or well-cut trousers and a blouse but make sure you look good, so you are ready for anything, anytime. Be at your most attractive self. You never know when or where you just might find yourself meeting the right man. If you look and feel great, you'll have the confidence to say hello. It also sends out the signal that you respect and value yourself. Those are very attractive traits and may help a lucky someone to strike up a conversation with you.

What attracts women is not the same as what attracts men. I know this to be the case because I've seen it reflected in the circulation figures of a magazine. Let me share a personal experience with you. Back in the early 1990's I edited one of the first ever sex magazines for women. I also edited a men's mag. The men's magazine did extremely well. The publishers assumed that a similar magazine aimed at the female market need only mirror the men's magazine. And so the style of the content and particularly the photographs were the same as for the male market. Big Mistake!! The publishers being men thought that what men wanted – women also wanted. So with brilliant fanfare announcing a new sexual revolution there were five sex magazines launched by different publishers all at around the same time. These featured explicit photographs of naked men. It was all billed as 'our turn to look'. All the magazines failed eventually. At its launch our new magazine sold upwards of 60,000 copies in the first month, this then dwindled to 25,000 in the next few months and eventually decreased to 5,000 copies before the magazine closed. This was women's 'turn to look' and women clearly didn't want to. The comparable magazine aimed at men had circulation figures of 250,000 every six weeks (18 publications in a year).

It may have been a contributory factor that the distributors, Menzies and WH Smith placed the women's magazines on the top shelf. The average height of a woman is 5'.3". She couldn't reach the top shelf but then she wasn't asking for help either.

At the time of the magazine's launch a survey was carried out amongst women on who were the sexiest men in Britain. The results revealed that the sixth sexiest was overweight comedian Robbie Coltrane. At around the same time a men's style mag printed a list of the women those male readers found attractive. Blonde and curvy Pamela Anderson was right at the top. I think it's pretty fair to assume that men have sex glands in their eyes and that women are just not as visually turned on as men. Yes of course this is a huge generalisation – but overall it bears out. My clients reflect this. Men when asked what kind of a woman they would like to meet generally identify visuals before characteristics. On the other hand women will ask for a man who takes care of his health, has financial stability, works hard and is funny and intelligent. There is an old saying that men sell love for sex and women sell sex for love. There is some truth in this. Men do need to be appealed to visually – it's in their make-up. A woman wants to be appealed to by intelligence. At first sight she is looking for protection, strength, and masculinity. He is looking for someone with visibly good genes to bear children. This gender difference is important in your strategy for meeting a man. Accept that attraction is important and keep that in mind when you work out two important factors:-

a) who you are and
b) what you are looking for.

Until those two things align, and you understand the difference then your chances of success are low. Does what you are looking for match who you are?

Because love can happen anytime anywhere you've always got to be ready for it. Chance is only a part of the meeting process – it doesn't cement without attraction.

And that means being your attractive best at all times. Making sure you are visually appealing. Nothing will happen if you are leaving the house without making an effort to be your most attractive self. But looking your best is not only done to attract, but it's also something you should do for yourself. By looking your best you are more likely to be feeling your best – and that exudes confidence which is also attractive. I have a friend who has the particular skill of knowing how to switch on her most attractive confident self. You can walk down the street with her, and she is unnoticed – and then she'll say watch this… and out goes the big bosom. She seems to stretch up taller, her walk changes to more of a sexy bottom swinging strut, and she smiles at everyone. Suddenly she stands out in a crowd – and men look at her admiringly as she goes past. She's giving off an appealing 'I'm sexy and confident' air.

## TIP

Get out of bed this morning and every morning and get dressed with this thought. This could be the day when I might just meet someone special. Look attractive, be attractive and think attractive. Just like my sexy friend. Couples often meet by an accident of fate. You may think – yes but I never do meet anyone. In this book you are going to learn how to increase your chances. How to double your opportunities and how to grab them when they come your way.

Chance is a wonderful thing because you really feel that something special has happened.

Some people don't believe in it. Like my 85-year-old uncle, Major Tony Fidler. He believed there was something more to it and he gave it a name. He called it the CBI – The Committee for Benevolent Intervention. The CBI is all the people who have loved you who have passed away. These people may be friends or relatives. Sitting round a table somewhere these 'angels' of ours convene to plot, plan and execute wonderful things to happen for our best interests.

Possibly it is the CBI who makes love happen. Perhaps they create the luck of being in the right place at the right time. That sliding doors moment that can happen to any of us at any time. The man for you could be drinking a coffee in the same café as you, sitting opposite you on the train, standing next to you even when you bought this book. We're often so busy being engrossed in something that we forget to look at who is around us. But when you do meet that person, you want to make sure you are looking your most attractive best – so you need to tick that attractive box most, if not all, of the time. The CBI won't want to be waiting for you to be looking your Sunday best.

Perhaps your perfect partner is an elusive type, hiding somewhere in a shady pub, strolling through streets unwatched, or deeply engrossed in some essential work or other. You don't know what he looks like, but you imagine he has immense intelligence and something beyond charm, beyond sexiness. You don't 'find' such a man – instead you wait until the CBI roll the dice, fiddle with chance, and execute their own plan for you. So always be ready.

There are so many incredible stories of how people have met. It's not unusual for it to happen while food shopping. Meeting a man in the local supermarket happens often but pick your supermarket to meet the man you want to meet. Supermarkets know this happens and they have been known to deliberately hold scheduled singles nights. It happened to Lucy. She got chatting to a man in dairy, it progressed in meat and by the time they met again in the drinks aisle he was asking her which bottle of wine she wanted with the dinner he was cooking her. Actually, she turned him down. He was a high-profile bodyguard and Lucy didn't fancy getting caught in any crossfire. The guy had recently returned from Africa having failed to preserve the life of his politician client. Seems he forgot to say "duck".

*How I Met My Man and How You Can Meet Yours*

But my favourite story of a chance meeting is this. It goes to show that love really can happen – anytime – anywhere – any place – and often when it is least expected. A dear friend of mine met her husband while she was picking up her groceries. This is her love story. My lovely, beautiful, captivating friend who I loved very much told me this and I am going to tell it how she told it to me. There is magic in it.

My friend - I'll call her 'S' - was standing in the grocery department of Harrods buying her provisions. No doubt she would be squeezing, sniffing, and carefully scrutinising even the smallest tomato for flavour. 'S' was a foodie - an excellent cook who always sought the very best ingredients for her dishes. Hence, she was out shopping in the food department at this most prestigious store.

Now 'S' knew the man who ran the fruit and veg department well and they were exchanging their usual banter about which tomatoes were best etc when he suddenly lowered his voice and asked if she recognised a man standing across the other side of the food hall. 'S' looked up and described to me later that what she saw was a distinguished man with a powerful face – like the strength you see in the features of a lion's face. I have seen this man in an interview on television. It was a compelling interview for all the reasons that 'S' immediately spotted. He was a creative man who had achieved a large body of famous work. 'S' had seen much of it and admired him. He's brought pleasure to millions worldwide across many generations. And she wanted to tell him. So this gracious extraordinary woman – with her striking posture and stunning

66

appearance - a complete one off – crossed the Harrods Food Hall to say hello and tell him how much she loved his work. She was genuinely delighted to meet him, and they spoke for half an hour. That should have been the end of the story, but no - love doesn't work like that.

Later that evening 'S' was at a friend's house for dinner. Eight people were invited but only seven were there. One guest was late. Very late. When he did arrive, he was a young man who came in quite flustered, full of apologies to his hostess. His late arrival and disruption though was soon forgotten because of what he said. *"I am sorry I am late, but I was having a drink with my Godfather, and he couldn't stop banging on about this woman he met in the grocery department today at Harrods"*. 'S' asked who his godfather was – and yes it was our man with the 'lion' like head. The connection was made, and the godson told 'S' that his godfather wanted to see her again. She said no. He was married. But actually, that marriage was reaching an end. Despite her protestations the very next day 'S' received a call. Much later on she became his wife and was with him until the day he died. There was so much love there.

I heard so many stories from her of their affection for each other and their amazing life together. He taught her much about his work and I have heard many of those stories. I have stayed in their house in Europe where you are surrounded by much of their creativity. It really was a meeting of two people who were destined to be together.

There is a prequel to this story that makes it even more weird. A month or so before 'S' met this man she went with a friend who wanted to see a female psychic. 'S' had only gone to the meeting to keep her friend company, but the woman insisted on speaking to her too. The psychic told 'S' that she needed to tell her something. A word. A name. The Christian name of a man. 'S' did not know anyone by that name, so she forgot about it at the time. It was the name of the man she would later meet in Harrods Food Hall.

I wonder if the CBI had picked out those two people to meet and share a portion of life together some time before. The upmarket grocery store was just a way of making it happen. By the way before you think – oh well she was beautiful so of course this would happen, then let me tell you that's not so. 'S' was not a conventional beauty. But she was unusual. Striking. And she very much made the best of what she was. She was hugely aware of herself and made the most of her presence in her walk and in how she held herself. 'S' had great shoulders and arm muscle definition, so her tops were always sexily sliding over one shoulder. She'd nailed her style and stuck to it. She put in the shop window the best things about herself, and she never, NEVER went out of the door looking anything other than her absolute best. If I rang her to say meet me in half an hour it wouldn't happen if she hadn't had her bath with beautiful smelling oils, if she hadn't made up her face, and chosen her clothes. I admire her for that alone. The world always saw her at her best. Even when she was just buying tomatoes.

*Delissa Needham*

It's an important thing to remember - Love can happen as a moment of Chance. Always be ready. Look and be the most attractive version of yourself so that whoever the CBI has picked out for you, that person will find you at your best.

## Chapter Six

# THE POWER OF CHEMISTRY.
# SMELL AND HOW IT WORKS FOR YOU.

There really is a chemistry to love.

The problem with online dating is that it's all too easy to look at a photograph of someone and then, in your desperately single state and full of hope, to trot all too quickly down a fantasy route. You start texting, exchanging messages etc and in that 'hopeful' process you become self-delusional. Being delusional is always present in any relationship because we impose on others what we want them to be, but in online dating we have no idea at all who someone is. Which is why meeting someone in the real world is so much more reliable. Because that enables your body to do its own quiet matching. You see, whilst we realise that there will always be a need for online dating, and it does serve a purpose, it's missing one crucial element in the process of falling in love.

Smell.

Until your computer has Smelly Vision or Scratch n Sniff, online dating will always be more miss than hit, because real attraction is in your nasal passages. Your body secrets a particular smell and it does so for a good reason. This smell is created by pheromones which are undoubtedly an important part of attraction. Pheromones are like hormones except they are busy on the outside of the body not the inside.

Sex pheromones act as messengers sending out signals to attract the opposite sex. These naughty little teasers are so confounding – they are the reason that very often you meet a man and have no idea why you are attracted to them, especially when they absolutely do not fit your idea of an attractive man. We are not just responsive to visual stimulation, but we also respond to olfactory stimulation. Pheromones are possibly present in all our bodily secretions but particularly in sweat which contains a particularly smelly compound called Androstadienone. It's usually found in its highest concentration in male body odour. And of course ever since it has been known that body smell stimulates attraction, various industries have grown up around the manufacture of pheromones. These apparently replicate the function of attraction created by real pheromones. Sometime ago I was sent a pack of pheromone sprays to try out. The results were not exactly convincing apart from the fact that the smells were unpleasant. At that time the science of pheromones was still relatively new and despite all the wild claims of making anyone seem attractive, the results told another story. I received two sprays, one for men and one for women. At the time there was no specific man in my life, so I used one spray on myself and the other on the dog. Did I pull? No. Did the dog pull? Well sort of but you never can tell with a dog. I mean he attracted the attention of a poodle in the local pub, but he may well have done that anyway. However all that masculine whiff did have some effect. He put his paw on the table, demanded a beer, got a sip of the dregs, and then tried to go into the Indian takeaway on the way home.

Perhaps the future for online dating would be to capture your own particular pheromone and send it to your blind date. If it doesn't smell right, he needn't bother.

Being attracted to someone is such a mixed bag of so many things. People have a sort of aura about themselves that can spark attraction. It's how people walk, talk, and hold themselves. How do you react to the way they move? What is your gut reaction to someone? These are such important things to consider not just what colour their eyes are or what they do for a living.

Your chemical make-up and your particular smell works to provide a potential mate with essential knowledge for the process of procreation. Your body is programmed to make sure you meet someone with whom you will ideally make a match and produce strong healthy offspring. If their genetic defaults are a disaster for reproduction with you then chances are your body won't like their whiff.

So blow your nose and breathe in the air next time you go on a blind date.

You may well have heard of Oxytocin from the role it plays in reproduction. It makes childbirth easier and is also released during breastfeeding. It also moves men's sperm so it's a crucial hormone for the continuation of the species. But it also has other vital roles. Oxytocin is the love hormone. Or the cuddle hormone or even the bonding hormone. You get bucket loads of it during sex – which is why scientists reckon women like a cuddle after sex. That's the pesky blighter that formulates those annoying and desperate words 'do you love me' ….. 'say you love me'…

Oxytocin is one of the three happy hormones that include serotonin and dopamine. Anything that releases those happy hormones of course makes us feel terrific and that happens when we're around people we like or feel attracted to.

It's not just sex that releases Oxytocin. Social bonding, social engagement or physical contact can release the hormone, which does go some way towards the reasons for inexplicable physical attraction. When released by a simple hug or a kiss it then in turn creates a reward rush. Even petting the dog can release Oxytocin. The interesting news is that research by endocrinologists has shown the impact of this hormone on monogamy because it regulates emotional responses. The more we are around people the more we do things that feel great and therefore the more oxytocin we release. And whenever you get more of that feelgood oxytocin rush the more you engage with the social and sexual relationship, and particularly with one partner.

And if you put on weight during Lockdown because as a single person you were comfort eating then blame your Oxytocin levels. The lack of it in certain areas of your brain will inhibit your ability to control eating and increase your eating impulses.

## Evelyn 35

I've always loved cars. I collected and sold several classic cars when prices started to rocket. Buying an old car at a cheap price and being able to sell it as a classic was a lucrative business for me during my Uni days. So when I once mentally compiled a list of the kind of man I would like to meet – a passion for similar things was important to of course and therefore cars too. So I did go to a few of those classic car shows and to classic car events like Goodwood and even to local car shows held in fields where anyone with a classic car would gather. But I never met anyone who wasn't a boring petrol head, so I gave up in the end. But then one day I was leaving an event and I did meet someone. But it wasn't in the best of circumstances. I'm sorry to say I was checking my lipstick when I ran into the back of another car. A police car. The policeman who got out was not cross – not his fault, not his car – but he did at least have a sense of humour. He walked over to my car and of course my heart was in my mouth. He knocked on the window and I wound it down. He asked me to turn off the engine and then said, "may I ask madam what you do to stop your car when I'm not here". I suppose if I hadn't been quite so cross with myself, I might have laughed but things were just about to get embarrassingly worse. The

*Delissa Needham*

officer asked for my licence, spoke into his radio, and discovered that my car tax was not up to date. At that point he asked to investigate the car boot. Now the thing was that I had been on a photographic shoot the week before and the props were still in the boot. Along with a pair of crutches left over from a routine foot operation. I had nowhere else to keep them and although my foot was now fine, strictly speaking I shouldn't have been driving for another few days yet. Embarrassingly the props in the boot were from a pornographic shoot. So thrown into the trunk was a pair of pink fluffy high heeled marabou slippers, a black lace corset trimmed with pink marabou and a pink feather boa. I'm a stylist. It's what I do. Search out props for shoots. I really was not keen on the officer looking in the boot and I think my reluctance was beginning to show. The officer found that somewhat suspicious and asked me again to release the boot. Oh dear. I was going to get done for driving without tax, but I was really hoping that the marabou slippers would be more interesting than the crutches. I just didn't want to be done for being unfit to drive as well.

Luckily the police officer looked at the items and not seeing a duffle bag of cocaine or a dead body shut the boot. Then told me I was not allowed to drive the car any further until it was taxed. However he conceded he would allow me to drive home, and he would take a statement at mine. It was at that point the officer said, "it's a shame we had to meet this way". I suddenly realised he fancied me. The feeling was mutual.

*How I Met My Man and How You Can Meet Yours*

Months later I saw him in my local pub, off duty. And yes, he did eventually ask me out on a date, and it was fun. In fact we dated for some time. It didn't really work out in the end, and I eventually moved down south but what a funny way to meet someone.

Cars do play quite a part in how couples have met. One woman met the man of her dreams when she took her car for repair. He was the dishy mechanic who was working on her undercarriage. Someone else met a man while buying paint in the trade paint shop. Another woman I know met her great love when she went to buy a car from the local dealership, and there are many stories of women who have crashed into someone and started a relationship. Like Pauline who drove her mini into the side of a Porsche when turning left in Park Lane. How she missed seeing a yellow Porsche who knows but the first words out of her mouth were "what do I have to do to get one of those then". Pauline could get away with that ... she was wearing a short leopard print skirt at the time and as her long legs untangled and emerged from the mini, I expect the Porsche owner blessed the day he was driving down Park Lane.

Shannon met a police officer while she was breaking the speed limit down the A12 in her Porsche. This was in the days when you didn't always automatically get booked particularly if you had a 32DD chest (yes this is a true story) and so Shannon did smile and push forward her valuable assets to get off the speeding ticket. She bumped into the same police officer while he was off duty in a bar a week late and that initial meeting led to a date and eventually to marriage.

*Chapter Seven*

# STOP MAKING THE WRONG LISTS AND START MAKING THE RIGHT ONES.

You need to be realistic about who you are hoping for. It's fine to dream but I'm here to focus you so you don't waste time.

You know the saying 'I want, don't get". Oh yes, she does, but when you want to meet a new man it's not practical to write down a hopeless list of wants. There are lots of women who create a list of specifications that would overload Amazon. Some even have a picture; I want one that looks like this (holding up a picture of George Clooney, or Idris Elba etc). We can only be that precise when looking for a new car or a tin of soup but not a human being. We have seen and heard many of those lists and they are all pretty much the same with women generally wanting the same specifics. So before we can make any progress together, we need to be very clear about what we are looking for and we need to be realistic. Cross a few things off the list and build a more sensible and specific partner profile. That way there is more chance of success.

I'm going to help you cut to the chase and make a real spec list – one that you can build your strategy from. Here's the top five I have heard time and time again. Read and decide if any of these specifics should be on your list, or if they should be binned on the grounds of unrealistic expectations.

## 1. I want to marry a rich man.

Oddly popular one! All over the world the rich elite arrive at glamorous destinations in yachts or private jets and head off to exclusive hotels or exotic homes. We have all met women who want that life and see their entry ticket as marrying a man with loads of money. If that's your ambition, then I am not here to criticise. But money doesn't buy you happiness - we are told. I'd like to be given lots and lots of dosh to test that theory out please. Seriously, if this is at the top of your list here are a few things to think about.

A wealthy, self-made chap is driven by the desire to make money. For some of them it's the means, the only means to enjoy life. He spends his money on expensive goods so the rest of the world can see how successful he has been. He buys the supercar, a large yacht, designer watch, more houses etc. All symbols of how well he is doing. The woman on his arm is therefore also a symbol of achievement, of success. She must be a woman of high value. A walking, talking Ferrari.

Unattainable to the average man. A woman who represents success. Are you that woman?

Show me a rich man who had bought himself an old banger and I'd say he was rarer than a real diamond in a Christmas cracker.

To be brutal, if all you want is to marry a rich man then you must have limited ambitions. I recommend you stop reading this book and go get yourself a degree in civil engineering instead.

Certain women have stock. Read any newspaper and we see coverage of the 'unattainable' women – from what they wear to where they eat, shop, live and earn. Who they dated, who they are dating and who they might date next? It fills (and sells) pages. It sells goods. The handbag worn by a celebrity, the dress by a princess, the haircut of an actress. These women all have power to influence others. It's a business. So how high is your stock? Are you a supermodel, famous singer, or a world changing businesswoman? In other words, do you bring kudos to the relationship? Are you already in the club? To marry a rich man you must have high stock, a track record or the ability to turn heads.

Or are you like the rest of us mere mortals? What we are saying is don't punch above your weight unless you can weigh into the ring with equal kudos.

Or drop that spec off this list.

There is a more practical money aim. Financial parity. It's not essential but it helps. A financial equal means that you can both feel comfortable. With that comes genuine independence, freedom, and hopefully real friendship. While having money is important, the real lasting ingredient is liking someone and being mentally and physically attracted to them.

## 2. I want to marry a man who is fit and healthy.

Are you fit and healthy? If not, then start working on it right now. If you become fit and healthy you will meet a man who thinks the same way. It's another aspect of self-investment. If you care about your wellness, then your stock will rise with others who do. It is likely that you will be more confident as a result of looking after yourself. This makes you more attractive to others. It's not a question of 'fat' or 'skinny'. It's about feeling good about yourself, whatever your shape or size. It's about being healthy. A man who takes care of himself will value someone who thinks the way he does about fitness and health, and it means he already relates to something about you. That's a good start.

## 3. I want a man who is intelligent.

As the vet said to me about my new puppy – that's about as clever as he will get.

You want a man who is intelligent? Emotional intelligence or bookish ways? EQ or IQ? In my view the two rarely meet to the same level in the same brain. Barristers, surgeons, lawyers etc all have an ability to focus with tunnel vision so that their minds are clear to absorb facts and data not emotional crap. The brain of a high IQ man is like a filing cabinet. The information he needs is easily accessible but there is no room in this careful ordered brain for emotional nonsense. But like I say that may just be my experience. What is important is to recognise the intellectual level that you enjoy. You will be bored stiff if you start dating a man who doesn't equal or exceed your own level of intelligence. Do you want to talk about the mundane? Do you want conversation that spins around who is doing what to whom, or do you want to talk about things that matter in life? Conversations about other people are the refuge of people who aren't very interesting. Conversely, it's no good dating a man for whom doing the crossword in Latin is a Saturday morning must do, unless you also enjoy Latin conundrums. Discussing Dante at the dinner table is great but not if you prefer to debate current affairs or the celebrity pages in your magazine. It's not wrong, it's just not compatible. So make a list of things you like to read, watch, talk about. It will help you to look in the right places. If you love discussing history then a history lecture or debate is going to be a more likely location to meet interesting people and potential partners. So intelligence definitely but focus on finding a partner that's your level. Preferably also with similar interests or your new relationship will be in the recycle bin faster than you can say subductisupercilicarptor (which is probably what you will do first).

## 4. I want a man who makes me laugh.

Now here's the thing. Comedians are some of the most intelligent people in the world. They have both high EQ and IQ. And be warned, they can laugh a woman's knickers off at 20 paces. "whoops there go my pants". Why are they so attuned? A comedian sees the world with an intense and rapid observation. Their brains move fast in the direction of humour. Laughter is an important part of our connection to each other. If two people from the same country meet anywhere in the world, the chances are that something funny like an observation or a joke will instantly unite them. Relationships often start that way and often power on thanks to laughter. We forgive someone who makes us laugh. We easily love those who make us laugh. It's a very powerful characteristic. But don't forget to look beyond it for the other personality traits. Humour like love can be blinding. Learn to look for what that humour and jollity may be hiding. People use humour to conceal real emotions and to ward off exposing too much about themselves. If you only fall in love with what makes you laugh, then you are at risk of eventually becoming a cropper.

## 5. I want a man who is attractive.

You don't really know what that is yet. You won't know until you see it. Your senses will know when chance throws the right man in your path. It may be that you have an immediate response as your heart skips that beat. Or maybe the attraction is a slow burner. The slow realisation that a friend has come to mean more, and you miss them when they are away. When you want to phone them about something funny that has happened. Be open to what you think you find attractive. You can't list attraction in your 'I wants' because too many other things will be more important to your subconscious. Like smell for instance.

Either adding in or taking out the top five from the popular list above means you should now be able to form a realistic list of your personal 'I want's'. What really matters to you. Write the two most important specifications down. If nothing else, it will stop you being blindsided by a devilishly attractive funny bloke who has nothing in common with you in all other aspects. Oh, if only I'd realised that sooner.

It has been said that marriage is a life sentence without a chance of parole. But marriage never starts with such cynical animosity. It begins with love and affection grown out of two people meeting. Like when Grace met Andrew:

How this love story gathered any speed at all mystifies me.

It happened in the Caribbean at 2a.m. under a bright full moon. During the day it gets so hot in the West Indies it's like God left the heating on but when the full moon shines in the Caribbean it's like God left the strip light on. Sometime in the early 1980's, Grace was strolling along a lane in the moonlight going the direction of the yacht club and heading for home after a party. The usual tropical sounds of frogs and cicadas were making a racket in the background. Walking with her was a nice boy called Simon, a deckhand from another yacht anchored stern to in the main harbour. Home for Grace was a yacht anchored out in a secluded bay in the south of the island of Antigua. This was Antigua before it became such a popular holiday resort. There were fewer yachts, less restaurants, few tourists and even fewer buildings and hotels. Grace was the chef on board a sailing yacht and normally she would have to be up and at work in just four hours, making breakfast for the crew of 6. But today was Sunday and there were no charter guests on board so no need to rise early. She and her co-worker, Daisy, had gone ashore for the evening and had agreed to meet at 2am by the dinghy dock to share the ride home. Grace was on time and there was the dinghy tied firmly to the dock and jostling with other dinghies for space. Daisy would no doubt be along in a minute and together they would be back on board in no time. Except there was one problem. As Grace and Simon stepped onto the end of the long dinghy dock, they both looked ahead into the distance and could see right at the end near Grace's dinghy was a man on top of woman doing – yep – having sex under the full moon right on the dock. Grace would actually have to step <u>over</u> the two lovers to get into the dingy. It was late, no one else was around. But the stage was well lit by the moon and the centre stage in her vision was a man's naked bottom. Grace assumed it must be Daisy underneath. So she retreated with Simon to sit behind the yacht club and wait for the couple to finish. Sitting just round the corner on the other side of the yacht club and talking in whispers was Daisy and her boyfriend. They both assumed it was Grace on the dock so were waiting discreetly for the dockside passion to subside.

85

*How I Met My Man and How You Can Meet Yours*

After a few minutes Grace heard the sound of a dinghy leaving the dock – someone was going home and then a minute later she saw a man walking past her from the direction of the dock. He paused for a second to light a cigarette, his face clear under the moonlight, and as he did so Grace recognised him as the English captain of the Swedish yacht anchored stern to in the main harbour. As he finished lighting his cigarette he looked up and saw Grace and their eyes met for a second. Grace smiled. He smiled back. Then off he strode. That was the chance meeting. Weird, isn't it? Years later their daughter asked Grace how she met her dad and Grace smiled and said that it was in a coffee bar. What else could she say?

I bet Grace had a list of 'wants' for an ideal husband but 'Daring Outdoor Shagger' was probably not on it.

*Chapter Eight*

# BE FOCUSSED BUT BE OPEN

The problem with not being open to suggestions is you don't really know what you are closing off from.

It's all very well having lists – they can help you focus. But if you are being too overly specific then you are not open to suggestions for what chance may bring you.

With this book I want to encourage you, to focus and to steer you, but I'm not going to con you by pretending it's all good news. The only good news will be the one you make for yourself with hard work and focus. And by not being as downright daft as Cheryl, a slim attractive woman recently divorced after 30 years of marriage.

Cheryl is reasonably well off and with her own home, lovely garden, and a nice income from investments – but she's on her own. She looked at online dating and didn't fancy it and her social life was not delivering any new single attractive and financially stable men. It was the usual stuff of tennis, bridge, golf etc. So Cheryl decided to go to an introduction agency. She knew what she wanted, and she was going to find an agency who would head hunt for her the kind of man who was her ideal.

She found the agency she felt was right and made an appointment to see Mrs X who ran this particular elite agency. Now Mrs X has seen some lists before, many with truly unrealistic items on it but Cheryl's list took the cake. On the list was the usual description of how she would like this particular man to look. For the 100th time Mrs X saw the Holy Trio (Tom, Matthew, George) and then under that was not a further description of the man Cheryl wanted but the specific information outlining the type of car he must drive. This was most likely above the detail 'must have own teeth'. Cheryl would have any man as long as he drove a Lamborghini. Who knows, but one thing is for sure that unless you can accept the man you fall in love with could well have bunions and drive a Fiat Panda you could well be putting your teeth in a glass of water before you are heading down the aisle.

If you strike off men for the smallest non-negotiable detail you will not be successful. Learn to accept you CAN live with a man who has fallen arches.

So Cheryl walked into an introduction agency waving a list of such ridiculous specifics, and then paid someone £12k on top of that to go looking for a needle in a haystack. She would have been better off hanging round a car lot – or better still going to car shows. If a car is so important you have to think

*How I Met My Man and How You Can Meet Yours*

of a cleverer way to meet the elite car owners. But really? Is that a goal for happiness?

Anyway Cheryl did find a man and fall in love - eventually. Having spanked £12k on nothing with Mrs X, she fell in love with her gardener. Yup doesn't that go to show that you can be as detailed as you want but it will all go out the window when love walks in through the door. The gardener was muscly and attractive, and he had a slow way of speaking but a gentle way of thinking. A kind, easy going man – but hot! And guess what he drove a bashed-up Ford Pick-up. Ha!

You need to adapt and be adaptable. Don't operate by stringent lists. Sure let them be your guide but not the immovable borders by which you define the only possibility of a romantic partnership.

But if you meet someone and it isn't right, move on. Don't push it. Learn to think more like you are speed dating. If it's not right don't keep flogging the dead horse hoping it'll get better or that you'll suddenly discover the man you are looking at has been hiding his light under an intellectual bushel and that the only reason he never reads a book is because he's already read every single literary work that ever mattered. If you crave to be with a man who is an intelligent thinker and this one isn't, then accept that and move on. If he's not an intellectual, then not much will change with him overnight. If there is a negative about a man you are attracted to then you had better examine how much that matters sooner rather than later. If something bothers you then it will only keep arising and it may just become the only thing you notice. If a relationship really isn't right don't waste time. Really DO NOT waste the time. You are only using up the time you could be spending looking for someone who really ticks the box more on the things that do matter to you in a long-term way. The person you get on with, click with, have good conversation with is the one you are most likely to enjoy having a long-term relationship with. The man who is tall, handsome, and rich and driving the right car could well be what you think is your ideal but how far will the relationship go if there's nothing to say.

Take our friend Deborah for instance. The first time she saw Roger he was leaning up the bar in the local hotel downing a pint. They got chatting and he asked if he could buy her a drink. She wasn't particularly fascinated by him, but she accepted, then he asked her if she would have dinner with him. For some reason that she doesn't understand she said yes and that was followed by another dinner. And on both occasions, she was bored but she went along with the flow. In the end she wasted 18 months with a guy knowing he wasn't right, but she kept going out with him time and time again. Visiting him for weekends and knowing that even after that first evening, she wanted to be miles away. She was bored but because she wasn't sure she would find someone else, she kept persevering.

Then one day she decided she couldn't take any more. She took a hard look at Roger and thought why am I wasting my time here?" I'm an intelligent woman spending time with a man who has nothing of interest to say. Deborah had finally realised that anything was better than this. If only she'd decided that much sooner. Deborah could have been looking for someone and she could have potentially found the right person by now. Instead she wasted 18 months. And let's face it – no girl needs to clock up time in the wrong direction. In that wasted time Deborah had put on weight and aged. What was the point of that? Planet Man is nearly always a place where a woman puts on weight and has less time to spend on herself. So it's not just the wasted time but the waste of looks that gets lost. If he's not right for you… don't hesitate….. ditch the dodo and move on.

One of the great things about being older is that we have knowledge, and experience. This should give us the power to make a decision more quickly than when we were younger and for the right reasons. If you move on now, there will be less hurt and more opportunity for both parties to find the right person. So be honest with yourself when going on dates. Time is so precious. We just don't realise it when we are younger.

You may also find yourself going in the wrong direction if you not only set out with the wrong 'must haves' but if you go hunting in a toxic pool. Every generation has a toxic pool, but particularly as you get older. It often happens that you may find yourself dipping into a social circle that has already been well mined for relationships many times over. Don't go to the same bars and the same hangouts as your existing social circle all the time, however safe this might feel. Don't go to bars that are deliberate pick-up joints. These are the kind of venues where you find women with a past engaging with men with no future. Bars filled with crusty old bachelors and general no hopers will only leave you feeling disillusioned. So avoid the toxic pool and make sure you go to places that are new to you and not just go to places that are jaded pick up joints. Being seen in such a venue can make you appear an easy pick up. If that's the message you want to convey fine – but it's not a good brand to peddle for a long-term relationship. A man once proudly told me that he never had a problem pulling women -as he is very well off and no dependents. I couldn't help but wonder who the women were to whom that basic list appealed.

That list would not have appealed to Alice who found love from a most unusual beginning.

## Alice 85

*"Pass me the scalpel"*. These were the first words Alice's future husband said to her. A short sentence and by no stretch of the imagination can this be considered a chat up line unless you are at a speed dating event for mass murderers. But this was followed a year later by another sentence "Will you Marry Me". That was over 60 years ago. Imagine if you met the man of your dreams over the open guts of a patient to the backdrop of gunfire.

This is Alice's story.

I was born in December 1937 exactly 4 years before the surprise attack by Japanese forces on Pearl Harbour, a US naval base near Honolulu, Hawaii. 2,400 Americans died in the attack. My older brothers Bob and Bill were killed. Both were in the US navy and were on board ship when the bombing happened. My parents lost 2 of their 3 children and so I was particularly precious to them. It was almost as though they couldn't bear it if I was away from home ever. I know they really hoped I would marry and settle in our hometown in the US state of Kentucky.

But I think I was influenced by the loss of my older brothers, and I wanted to feel that like them I was doing something with my life that mattered, but I also wanted to do something that I felt would set right the grief and loss my parents had suffered. So I trained as a nurse working for some time in a general hospital and eventually working in surgery. In 1965 I went with the Medical Corp out of Vietnam. My parents must have been so upset and so worried.

Anyone who has seen the great actor Alan Alda in Mash, the American comedy series that depicted life in a Mobile Army Surgical Hospital during the Vietnam War, will have some idea of what my life was like. An elite group of surgeons and nurses were living and working in a makeshift field hospital close to the battle. Helicopters would bring in the wounded and emergency operations were carried out to the backdrop of the noise of battle.

Two months into my tour of duty and I had become hardened to some of the worst of it. Most days I was in surgery - I hugely admired my colleagues and got on with everyone. Just like in Mash there was a lot of flirting going on but although I wasn't

*Delissa Needham*

short of admirers I wasn't interested. I was focussed on my career. Not love. But then love is always only a heartbeat away. Well actually it was just a jeep's journey away because driving into the Field Hospital one afternoon arriving at the same time as an ambulance of casualties was a young surgeon called Phil. He was to be stationed at the Field Hospital but literally as he arrived so did the casualties, so he was thrown in at the deep end and went straight to work scrubbing up with the rest of the surgical team to perform operations on some of the most severely wounded. Within a short time of arriving at the hospital Phil was gloved, gowned, and masked ready to operate on a young soldier with a bullet wound in his side. The anaesthetist was already at work, and I was the nurse assigned to the operation and to help the newbie surgeon. He stood one side of the patient and I the other side. I was very impressed with how he worked. Very precise, very calm. There was a moment when I thought we might lose the patient and I remember looking at Phil across the operating table. I suppose I was searching his eyes for any sign of worry. This was our first meeting and it led to a marriage that lasted nearly 60 years until Phil died last year. He was my love. My friend and my soul mate for all that time. I feel so honoured to have known him.

***

Alice and Phil met in unusual circumstances. But it goes to prove over and over to me and hopefully to you that you never know when love will turn up, where it will come from. So you must never give up hope. Never give up expecting. Never give

95

up trying. Never give up looking. Never give up flirting. Never give up looking your best.

# PART 3: STRATEGIC THINKING

*Chapter Nine*

## **WHERE TO LOOK.**

I have an important rule that I find invaluable.

It is…Turn up.

That's it. A very simple rule. Turn up.

If you are invited, don't procrastinate – just go. Aim to meet and engage with at least three people. You are aiming to take the conversation to a level where you exchange details with at least three people. It does not have to be a man. You are aiming to meet people. Meeting people leads to meeting people. What's your aim? To meet the person of your dreams. To meet them, then you need to be there. Simple as that.

So turn up. It gives you a chance to practice your conversational skills. To engage. Like anything in life, it takes practice to become proficient. It may have been a while since you have had any more social interaction than with your dog. You may find it intimidating, especially after a bad breakup, but please remember that there are others in the same position as you. You may meet them and find common ground. Give others a chance. Don't write off an evening even if you dread it, or if it seems the most mundane of invites. Make the best of it. Find the positive.

If nothing else, by turning up it gives you the opportunity to dress up. What's the point in having nice shoes or a pretty dress if they never see the light of day?

Turn up. The aim here is not to meet a man. That kind of hunt is blatantly obvious and off putting. You are looking to engage with people. Do that successfully and in all probability, you will have success in meeting the right man. Hopefully someone surrounded by a social network that you recognise and are comfortable with; one with connections with the community that you are involved with. Isn't that preferable to meeting and putting your trust in some stranger you came across on the internet?

So turn up. The more people you meet, then by turn the more people you meet, therefore increasing your chances of meeting the right guy. It's just maths.

You must be proactive if you want to meet someone. If you have decided that you want to meet someone new, then don't leave it to chance? If you want a holiday, you start looking at places to go; want a new house, you visit new areas, and do your research. Why should looking for a partner be any different? Why is chance seen as romantic but diligent application be seen as unfeminine. If you choose to spend more time choosing a moisturiser than a date, what do you expect to happen?

So think smart.

Turning up is one thing; thinking smart is another.

Don't be lazy. You wouldn't in your daily life, so why would you be here? Men don't hide down the back of a sofa like an old coin; they are busy with interests and activities that they enjoy. There are most likely hundreds of hobbies and leisure activities, venues and opportunities going on in your town? How lucky you are that there are so many opportunities. This is the great advantage you have that your mothers and grandmothers didn't have. For them, socialising with the hope of meeting a man would be limited to being invited to meet someone at a friend's house, or a bridge party, or local bingo, church, or the village hall dance. That was probably it. In your grandmother's heyday, finding anyone who was not in her immediate environment and therefore already known was pretty slim. There simply wasn't the opportunity to look far and wide. So how lucky are you. The world's your oyster and it's searchable with a 'click'.

Employ a researcher if you need to. If you are in a big city plenty of things are happening and much of it is written about. If you are living in a more remote area there are still local papers, internet sources and of course, friends who always have the answer so ask. Someone always knows someone who may have the answer. A recent friend has had to move due to a breakup. It's some distance from everyone she knows, but already she has found a walking group, dog training school and wild swimming (who knew?). Yes, it's rural but that's where she wanted to go. It's a start.

When Flora decided she wanted to meet a new man she was methodical about it. Flora decided she would do every hobby in her area from A-Z until she met someone. She found Peter during her 'R' time (rowing). It was an exhausting process. If she had profiled her ideal man first and had been more focused, she could have gone straight to 'R".

You could do the A-Z approach, but good luck with Bowls and Fishing. R also stands for Reeling, so if you like being thrown about by men in kilts, go for it.

Here's a comparison to thinking outside the box. It's a clever example of using a strategy to achieve a goal. It's about a person who is now a famous actress. Back in the early 1980's she was an impoverished young drama student, just out of RADA and no job. Rather than struggle to get auditions, she got a job as a secretary. Her employer was an acting agent. Clever hey? Kate sent herself on auditions. That's how she got ahead of the competition.

Success depends on how much you are prepared to do to be successful. I know of women who have gone to great lengths to be in the right place. On a Thursday night in the City of London there are two streams of people, those going home after a long day in the office and those coming in, dressed up to enjoy time with those who have worked a long day in the office. Everyone is heading to the many hostelries that the City has to offer. Sure you can join an exclusive club and try and pick the right days and the right times when the single men are about, or think smart like another friend. She got herself a job running the bar at her local golf club. She didn't need the job, but she did want to meet someone. What better way to do it? At some point most of the members of the golf club spent time in the bar. And there she was. Bingo!

Some women I know have given serious thought as to what they want to achieve and have come up with novel ways of putting themselves in the right playground to meet someone. One woman took up shooting. She was wealthy and she bought Purdey guns, a sexy Westwood tweed suit and got herself invited to a shoot. It's a high-end game but that strategy is applicable across the board. We all know the story of the famous actress who took up golf and met a famous actor on the golf course. She is now happily married to Hollywood royalty.

Are Rugby players your type? Does your local rugby club need help? Fund raising, organising tours, helping with events? There is so much you can do to engage in your town, meet new people and do a good turn while you are at it. Who wouldn't like a woman who helps fundraise or provide cricket teas or help with the elderly (who knows who might be visiting)? Jenny's local sailing club does disabled sailing days. She loves sailing and helping out. There's a lot of interesting people at the club and it has a busy social calendar. It's not rocket science, nor is it calculating: You have to start somewhere.

Decide on who you want to meet, focus on where it is and then go out - get involved.

If you think the same way as all the other single women hoping to meet a man, then you are going to be another goldfish peering out from an overcrowded aquarium. How do you stand out, get noticed and start those conversations? Success is being where other women are not. You have to find the man you want on his own turf, when he has time to notice you. His playground if you like. Not in traditional territory where everyone is either hunting or hunted.

From rugby to supermarkets, men are out and about. Whether it's on the train, jogging in the rain, buying meat for the barbie, buying the beers, or standing in a gallery, they are there. So be imaginative. Remember that our friend working the bar at the golf club didn't need the job? Get out and about because your objective is to meet new people. The right man will surface eventually.

If you find yourself a good and talented research person, they should be able to create a list of likely events for you that will keep you busy for some time. They should know the area you live in, think creatively, and know how to get access to the events you are interested in. One who comes with exclusive access to any members only clubs or with friends who run social diary pages, listings, or venues. My dating team has sent our clients to lawyers' lunches, magazine launches, book readings, lectures, exhibitions, exclusive parties, political marches (why not?), hospital events, race meets, local resident committees, church fetes, farmers markets, auctions – we could go on and on. That's before you think about sports clubs, drinking events, food fairs etc. One of our friends met her new squeeze whilst discussing chard on a Sunday. He was a farmer and she loved cooking. She kept running into him every week at their farmers market and they'd talk about vegetables and cooking. Eventually she invited him round to see what she could do with a simple parsnip.

<u>Tip</u> If you want to meet someone in the real world and not online then get out there. Speak to everyone and anyone. And please don't tell yourself that you don't have time. I have heard clients say that – in the same breath as telling me they've recently watched a box set.

Dolly has always been happy to speak to everyone and anyone. She went to a ticketed event at lunchtime and got talking to a woman who became a new friend - Lucy. They met a couple of times for coffee or a drink. Lucy then decided she would organise dinner for six of her friends to introduce Dolly to her recently single male friend, Josh. The supposition being that Dolly and Josh had much in common and would no doubt fall in love and ride off into the sunset. What happened was very different from that sunny outcome. Dolly sat at the table with the other guests and waited with anticipation. Josh was late. An hour late. He was tall, good looking with his own hair and teeth but they did not get on. In fact, in next to no time, it was full blown war at their end of the table. Dolly had never met anyone she disliked more. However, Dolly did get on with one of the other men at the table, Hamish. This proves two things.

105

1) Meet people and you will meet other people. 2) Matchmaking is a tricky business.

Let's talk about pets for a moment. Who needs tinder when you have a dog? But only, ONLY if you own one already. I absolutely do not suggest that you get a dog to get a man. That would not only be thoughtless and stupid, but you would be unlikely to be successful if you didn't want the pet in the first place. People who love dogs love other people who love dogs. If you are not that type, then don't pretend to be. Other dog owners can sniff you out like they've got their nose on your bum. People who own dogs have dog conversations and they talk easily to each other. Dog owners meet other dog owners. There seems to be an inherent belief that if my dog gets on with your dog, then we will get on. Strange but true. 101 Dalmatians can't be wrong.

So however you want to do it, primarily you must expand your network. Don't rely too much on luck and chance. The adage that the harder one works the luckier one gets is as true in the dating game as much as anywhere else.

## Alison 35

I suppose you could say that how I met Paul was straight out of 101 Dalmatians. It was a bit like how Roger and Anita met - and of course how Pongo and Purdey met. Like Anita I was a happy singleton and definitely not looking for love. I was perfectly ok being just me and my lovely terrier Stanley - sometimes known as the 'Little Sod '. At the time I met Paul I had just moved from London to a quiet Cotswold village to be near my sister and her children. I'm a freelance journalist and author so I can work from anywhere. I moved at the start of the summer so it couldn't have been better timed. The hedgerows were filled with pretty flowers, the rolling hillside was beautifully green, and it was a good summer. Warm and sunny. I usually got around places on my bike. There's a huge basket on the front and Stanley likes to sit in it, leaning back like he's in an armchair, his little button eyes taking in the world while I do all the hard work of peddling. On the day I met Paul, I was in my yellow flowered frock and on my bike with Stanley in a quiet country lane. As I turned a corner the lane ahead ran gently downhill and as we progressed the bike gathered pace. At the bottom, the front wheel hit a dip and a rocky stone and suddenly I was catapulted off the bike and into a hedge. Thankfully Stanley was ok. I had to crawl out of the hedge the way I was facing which meant I was in somebody's garden. It was a very pretty garden and scattered across the large lawn were tiny dead bodies. Stuffed dog toys. A scruffy rabbit here, a torn penguin there, a stuffed bear with an ear missing, a pink pig lying on its back with its trotters in the air etc. Sad little creatures that appeared abandoned but then out of nowhere came another terrier, barking furiously. Stan had just crawled through the hedge after me and I think for him it was definitely love at first sight. The other dog was the same breed as Stanley which is quite a coincidence as you don't see many of his breed. If I was a dog, I would adore Ruby at first sight. She was a pretty dog with almost the same markings as Stanley. There was a lot of immediate tail wagging

*How I Met My Man and How You Can Meet Yours*

and then an introduction to the deceased toy collection. I was keen to get out of there - I was feeling stupid and I was in a private garden but of course Stanley had other plans. I hissed at him to come back but being in 'Little Sod' mode, Stanley had better things to do. Then the owner of the garden came out of the doors of the house. I sort of recognised him. I thought he was a novelist. Turns out I was right. I think I must've been such a sight. I realised there was a bit of hedge in my hair and my knee was bleeding. Paul and I often recount this story to each other, adding bits of detail over the years. Ruby and Stanley completely ignored us and got on with their own 'thing' while Paul rescued my bike from the hedge, sat me down with a cup of tea and even sorted out my grazed knee. So that's how we met. As Paul often very sweetly says "It's not often that a garden hedge sprouts girls". The right hedge at the right time for Alison.

The same kind of accident with a happy ending happened to Jane. Except she was on her way back from a Charity Ball in her battered car, an old Ford Capri.

## Jane 43

It was two in the morning, and I was crossing Suffolk in early winter dressed in a ball gown with long diamante earrings and a sparkling necklace. The roads were icy, and I was driving carefully but I didn't account for a patch of black ice on a double bend. The car skidded and I drove into a box hedge in which was buried a high plinth of rock. Scary when I think back. It could have been so much worse than it was. The Ford

Capri, still going at speed, climbed the plinth and came to a halt on top where it balanced rocking back and forth with me, very shaky, still at the wheel. I am not kidding you when we tell you that what happened next was the start of my 20 year marriage ....and counting. The hedge surrounded a beautiful Georgian house recently inherited by the man I was about to meet - Marcus. A city stockbroker who was at home for the weekend. He was woken by the sound of my Ford in trouble, he got up, went to the window, and drew back the curtains. We often laugh about this now. There was I, looking back at him in my diamante earrings and fine evening gown, behind the wheel of a Ford Capri balanced precariously on his box hedge.

\*\*\*

These things happen. It could happen to you. But it won't if you sit on the sofa. It won't if you wait. It won't if you don't get out and meet people.

So, TURN UP.

*Chapter Ten*

# HOW TO NETWORK FOR DATING.

Get Networking

Get off the sofa, get out there and get meeting people.

I recognise that social media has a role to play in meeting people, but you also need to be out in the real world. The more people you meet the more chances of meeting the one you've been wanting to meet. If you spend too much time on the sofa with the telly and that comforting bottle of wine, then eventually you will become less interesting and less interested. Your ability to engage in conversation gets out of practice as does your ability to listen. If this is you then I recommend you do what my friend Elizabeth did. She bought an excellent new television, watched for a few nights, and then a week later took it back to the shop. The shopkeeper asked her what was wrong with it. There was nothing wrong with it — just that she kept watching it. Yep! What's wrong with the TV is that you'll watch it. The epitaph on your park bench will read 'No one really knew her. She was too busy watching TV'. If you start watching that 24-episode drama series then that's 24 hours of your life - gone. 24 hours you could've spent meeting people while learning how to sail or joining a group of strangers listening to a political debate.

To grow your network you must want to engage with people. Learn to listen. Don't talk about yourself but ask others about themselves. Everyone has a story, and everyone has something of interest to say about themselves or their experience in life. Being a person who listens and engages in conversation makes you good to be around. That in itself will expand your network.

Don't keep repeating a fixed agenda i.e Monday is Bridge night, Tuesday is choir night, Wednesday is Tennis night etc. Expanding your network by meeting people who are not in your immediate circle. If you genuinely want to increase your chances of meeting someone then you need to grow your network – not stick to the same one.

Be fun and outgoing if you can, and if that's not you then learn to demonstrate interest by asking questions. And I recommend you keep your political opinions and your 'causes' under your hat for now. Have your heated debates with close friends not with strangers. There are some subjects that people are so passionate about they are incredibly divisive. Which is fine but not when growing your network. My recent experience is proof of this. I recently had the shortest date in my life thanks to political differences. The 'ideal man' (the one described by the mutual friend as "perfect for you. You'll fall in love with him") had barely parked his bum before he said something I didn't agree with. And he didn't agree with my response. So he tossed the hand grenade back over the tablecloth and I chucked it back by which time my voice had gone up so many octaves I was a barely audible squeak. I even wagged my waggy finger at him. Did I loathe Mr Perfect? If that man was the only other person on my shipwrecked island, I'd make a boat out of an old cornflake packet and row as far away as possible. Is there a time and place for politics? I think we can surmise that there is. But although it's not a great way to grow your network at least a fiery response is being true to yourself and your beliefs. Your choice.

<u>Tip</u> if someone says to you, "you live in Basingstoke? I have a friend who lives in Basingstoke, I must introduce you". Grab the offer. Don't let it slide, especially if you are new to an area. Ask if you may forward an email or contact details so they can be passed on. Ask to be put in touch. Be positive about it. Be proactive. Most people are willing to help if asked, so make sure you do. You have got to meet as many people as you can. Tell people you've moved to Amazing Basingstoke and ask if they know anyone there. When you meet anyone new you don't have to form lasting friendships, but you may meet other people through that connection. You may also discover coffee shops, walks and meeting places. You could hear about new events and generally other things to do. So be bold, ask and push. Seize the opportunities.

Unless, of course, all that talk about meeting a new man is just...well.... talk?

Do you really want to meet someone, or is it a half-hearted wish and really you're quite happy to spend your evenings watching romantic comedies and wondering why Matthew McConaughey hasn't knocked on your door?

*Chapter Eleven*

# WHAT DO YOU WANT? REALLY, REALLY WANT?

Let's put this wish of yours under the microscope and find out just how real it is. Hands up if you agree with any of these statements.

1. I don't bother to notice men.
2. I don't care if men don't notice me.
3. My efforts to find a new partner extend to going out with my girlfriends to the nearest pub.
4. I can't be bothered to go out. It's raining. It's cold. There's probably a South Westerly wind coming.
5. I do not use my downtime to think of where I can make new friends and possibly meet the man of my dreams.
6. I over rely on my immediate friends for intros and invites.
7. I never flirt or bother to be engaging.
8. I can't be arsed to look my best, so I don't bother with beautification (manicures, makeup, hair dye etc).

9. I have a great time with my dog, my hens, my budgie, my llama, my bottle of wine so I don't need a man. (Good on you but we're not refunding your money).

If you do not notice men, then you either don't want one or can't be bothered. Otherwise open your eyes and look at every man you see.

If men do not notice you then you need to up your game until they do. Living life in the natural state is comfortable and cheap but if you don't show investment in yourself then why would you expect anybody else to do so. Showing up at a friend's party still in your dog walking outfit complete with wellies and a pocket full of poo bags may be a sign that you are an old friend, but it's not going to win you admirers. And unless your hostess also has a whiff of dog about her, and you don't want to upstage her with a whiff of Chanel I'd say it's disrespectful to not bother to smarten up. I remember when I first bought a house in the country and invited my London friends for lunch. To a man they turned up in old jeans and trainers as if I'd left my sense of style and love of clothes at the county border. It's the equivalent of those women who go on holiday to a tropical island and leave their much-needed bras at Heathrow airport. I don't think British Airways have yet offered a bust lift with the inflight entertainment.

Don't rely on going out with your girlfriends in the hope of meeting the right man. It's scary for chaps to try and break into a pack of girls and besides lots of other women are trying

*Delissa Needham*

the same strategy. You need to be more exclusive in your thinking.

Do not rely on friends to introduce you to a potential single man. It's great if they do, but it's not without risk for the mutual friend. Potentially they could lose two friendships if it goes wrong. Also, it's an uncomfortable fact that your married friends may not prioritise mixing with singles. Couples like couples. Apart from many other reasons it makes the seating arrangements easier for dinner parties. A round table anyone?

Flirting is fun and can be charming. I have a friend who could flirt with a chair if she needed to. Flirting is a much-maligned activity. Yes, it can be sexual, but it can also be playful, fun and makes people feel better. Male and female, young and old. You remember people who flirt with you. It's a type of humour. One of my neighbours drove past me the other day in a brand-new blue Porsche. Next time I saw him walking his dog I said, "Harry it wasn't til I saw you in that car I realised how handsome you are". Flirty fun.

Do beautify and pamper yourself. First of all, you will feel better. More in control, more confident. Even that in itself is a great thing. Secondly, feeling attractive leads to being attractive. Even if it's just getting your nails painted. A little bit of pampering makes you feel special.

I wish I had money for every woman who says they want a boyfriend but when I drill down, I find that the sum total of their efforts is to peruse the latest popular dating site. I can't say it enough that if you want to meet someone you need to get out into the real world and head towards the kind of venues, locations, and activities where you are likely to meet the man you want to be with. Let me repeat my favourite mantra..... the more people you meet the more you are likely to meet the one you want to meet.

Here's a thing NOT to do. This one thing that will get in the way of networking, meeting new people and totally hold up your chances of meeting your perfect partner. An affair with a married man. DO NOT date a married man. Avoid like the plague. It's destructive, unhygienic (yup – why else is he showering before he goes home?) and a waste of time. No matter what rubbish he spouts. Would you like it done to you? If a marriage is missing some basic element, then you are just topping up the jam jar, adding butter to the mash etc. There will be no change in the situation until there is a catalyst. Do you want to be that catalyst? You may not win the guy in the end if you're just the catalyst. And then actually you may not want him. Who wants someone who cheats? Wait until the divorce goes through. Be a friend until it does but don't be the one who is the Band-Aid. Remember what happens to Band-Aids. Once the healing is done, you're in the waste bin.

Take Rosie for instance. She met a nice guy called Charlie through her new job. They got on really well and ended up leaving a work social event together. One thing led to another. And in no time at all they had joined a knitting circle and created the world's longest scarf? No... they ended up at her place at 2am eating chocolate flavoured granola. Then the shenanigans began. The illicit 'see you in the stationary cupboard... bring your own cereal bowl'. Charlie was married and had taken full advantage of his night out. Home was a nice house, two children and a dog, but there just wasn't enough going on in the bedroom. To get to his wife he had to get past a large glass of wine and a bag of chips. He's had affairs before, so Rosie wasn't the first, but she didn't know about the others, and besides he said that he loved her. So that was fine then? Charlie told Rosie that he and his wife were separating. Unfortunately, he forgot to tell his wife that crucial information. Why would he? Firstly, in this tale of woe follow the money. If Charlie and his wife sold the family home the most they would be able to afford separately would be a flat each. Secondly, family is family, and that unit is a supplier of great strength. Being judged by your children as a homewrecker is not easy. Besides, he liked his wife. She made him laugh. She knew him and all his idiosyncrasies. It was familiar, it was safe. For Rosie time was marching on. Her dream of starting her own family was receding into the distance as her egg count was going down faster than Sainsburys at Easter. Hanging on to the offcuts of someone else's life, no big celebrations together, a life in limbo. Time that could have been spent finding a man for her. Totally for her.

Eventually the dam burst, and the wife found out. Charlie realised what was important and it wasn't Rosie. That's probably the oldest story in the book.

*How I Met My Man and How You Can Meet Yours*

Lucy on the other hand was only ever interested in one specific type of man and she was very focussed about achieving her wish.

## Lucy - late 40s

I've always fancied cricketers. I don't really know why. Is it something to do with their gentle manners, that languid posture or is it the way they rub the ball. Who knows? I like my men tall and elegant and very often those features are in a cricketer. I was tired of being on my own and I hadn't had any success with the usual routes - dating agencies, friends' intros etc. So I decided I needed to formulate a plan to meet a cricketer. A friend knew a cricket team who played regularly around the South East so she wangled me an invite to join the team for cricket tea. In no time I did meet a guy I liked, and I ended up joining him at various cricket matches. He was nice enough but to tell the truth I wasn't bowled over. Nevertheless, I hung on in there and eventually I met another cricketer, Jeremy. He was from an opposing team and he and I got on very well. It was great and we went out for a while but again it didn't really set me on fire. Anyway we still went on holiday together – to a friend's villa in the South of France for 14 days. Unfortunately (or not) Jeremy had to return home sooner for business, but I stayed on for the remaining 3 days. Now it gets weirdly coincidental. I got off the plane at Heathrow and walked into the luggage hall. I located the number of the carousel expecting to deliver my luggage and went over to it and waited. Soon the luggage started to arrive,

*Delissa Needham*

piling on to the moving belt at one end and eventually arriving in front of me, and passing. Other people collected their bags and disappeared, but my luggage didn't arrive. Then finally I saw it pop out between the plastic strips and plop with a bump onto the carousel. A big blue double pocketed Brics holdall – an expensive gift from Jeremy to me especially for the holiday. I remember I walked round to collect it and as I reached out for it so did someone else. A man who said" I think you'll find that's mine". He had dark hair, glasses and amusing eyes set in a thin attractive face. I was pretty sure he was wrong so straight away I said, "no I think you'll find it's mine". The bag went onto the ground and the man bent down to open the bag and prove it was his. He pulled back the zip to open the holdall and I was praying my dirty lingerie hadn't somehow made it to the top of the contents. But the first thing I saw was not my blue summer dress, or my espadrilles but a creamy white cricket jumper sticking out and under that was a pair of cricket trousers. Meanwhile going round the carousel and now leaving me was another blue Brics bag. Obviously mine. The man saw it and went to grab it for me. What then happened was a quick apology but that wasn't the end of it because he was going in the same direction as me out of the baggage hall and towards the queue for taxis. Naturally we chatted while we waited. Turned out he was going into London for the night before flying out to the West Indies for a cricket match in Barbados. This was no ordinary cricketer. He was a pro. I had been to Barbados to watch cricket two years earlier. On another occasion on a flight home from the West Indies a stewardess with a sense of humour had allotted me a seat in the middle of the entire All Stars Barbados Cricket team. Anyway, it turned out we were going into central London, so it made sense to share a taxi. I got out near my flat and he continued on to his hotel but not before he asked me if he could buy me a drink that evening. It was by that weird route that I found my perfect cricketer. It was a per chance meeting and now we are happily married and have children. Two boys. Both cricketers.

*Chapter Twelve*

## HOW TO LOOK GOOD AND THE PLEASURE OF MEETING NEW PEOPLE.

So you are finally out of the door. On your way to opportunity. Whether big or small. You're going out. You're all made up, you're wearing something that flatters you, your tights are not laddered, and your hair is brushed. Crucially there are no bits of hair where there shouldn't be and definitely no grey hairs -unless you're planning on dating Father Time. You've risen to the challenge, peeled off the track pants and hopefully you look like an Audi on a forecourt of Ford Fiesta's. Now what do you do when you get there? It takes a brave soul to walk into a room alone so get your head up, smile big, breathe, and enjoy the moment. Forget the traumas of your day. If the cat was sick on the carpet earlier in the day, well that's now behind you. Unless you left it where you found it. You are about to meet new people. It's exciting! What's the worst that can happen to you? That you are left standing on your own in a room full of people, feeling like something the

*How I Met My Man and How You Can Meet Yours*

cat sicked up? If that happens then you put one foot in front of the other, go up to the most accessible group (i.e not two people deep in conversation), put out your hand and say "hi, I'm Suzie". It's that simple. Crucially you must enjoy the pleasure of meeting new people with the knowledge that EVERYONE has something interesting to say.

Always put your phone away when you go to a party or event. Put it on silent/vibrate. You may need it instantly if you want to take down a number. The easiest way to do that is to voice memo record. And other than that don't use your phone. You can't meet and engage with people if you are busy sending that last email for work. Do it later. Anything less is rude to those around you and essentially you have to focus on the here and now. No distraction, no excuses. You are here to meet people, face to face and to grow your network of people. So focus.

Don't drink too much. It's never attractive. Eat something before you go out. If the canapes are going past you don't want to be busy stuffing food in your mouth. It's not a good look and you're here to meet people not sample sausage rolls. So side swerve that mini burger and teensie fish 'n' chips. You can always have a Big Mac on the way home. Many times I've stood in the queue for a burger in my diamante and evening dress.

If you are going to a location that's new to you then do research the journey. How are you getting there? If you need to park or take public transport, then how far will you be from the venue. You want to avoid a long walk in your high heels

124

and if it's hellish weather it might wreak havoc with your hair. You don't want to walk into the party looking like the lead singer of an 80's rock band. If you know where you're going you are more likely to arrive on time and be naturally relaxed, which is more than you can say for any 80's rock band.

If you are on a date, try to be prompt. Don't let the logistics of your journey make you late. It's a bad start if you keep your date waiting for half an hour because you didn't think about the traffic. Calling from your house pretending to be in your car when you haven't left the house just puts you under unnecessary stress. I know cuz I've done it often enough. Unfortunately on one occasion the house phone rang in the background when I was mid-call on my mobile telling a bunch of whoppers about the bad traffic in the high street.

If it is a completely new environment you are walking into, then it's even more important that you feel your best. Treat yourself to something that makes you feel good. Perhaps a new lipstick, perfume, underwear. If you feel good, you will be positive. If you are positive, more people will want to talk to you. That's the aim of going out right?

If this was a business meeting or a gathering of your book club you would have a common interest to fuel the conversation. In a varied social gathering you have no idea initially where you might find a commonality with anyone you meet. You have to find it, so the more you talk, and actually listen, to someone the more you are likely to find something in common.

*How I Met My Man and How You Can Meet Yours*

Here's your goal. At an event you must engage with a number of people but aim to reach a level with at least three people where you have exchanged names and even contact details. It is likely to be where there is a mutual interest in something/anything.

So now you are at an event. What next? You need the Art of Conversation.

The Art of Conversation indeed. What piffle. It's not like you're about to paint a Monet by dipping your brush into dialogue. I have to say these things though otherwise I'd be writing a very, very short book on how to meet a man and it would go something like this. 1) Open your eyes. 2) step out the door and 3) open your mouth and speak. Which is about the gist of it but unfortunately on that basis I'd soon be facing lawsuits from angry single women everywhere who would feel somewhat short changed.

So here it is. The Art of Conversation.

First things first. If there is a host at the event i.e. you've been invited to a party, then say hello to the host. Hopefully you've had the forethought to take a small gift. There will be a reason that you've been invited and hopefully it's not just to make up numbers. (However, if you are the only guest in the room then quite likely it is). Don't take up your host's time by expecting them to introduce you to everyone at the party. And don't make a beeline for the first single male you see. It's not cool. Hopefully your host will introduce you to someone at which point grab the intro with both hands to allow your host to go back to greeting their other guests.

You are now on your own with a stranger at a party. So smile and get the ball rolling. Hopefully your host has introduced you with a bit of detail i.e *"you must meet Suzie she's in PR"* or *"meet Mike, he's a chef"*. Or if you are lucky, *"meet Harry, he's an Acrobat in the Circus"* or *"this is Melanie, and she drives an HGV lorry"*. All good starters for a conversation. If you end up with "meet George; he's a software engineer", then best of luck, but then hey everyone on this planet has something interesting to say. Perhaps he's an expert in cleaning cat sick off the carpet.

Others may be as nervous as you might be so prioritise putting other people at ease. Politely and gently ask people about themselves and unless you have a comedy act to rehearse, don't begin the conversation with a "funny thing happened to me today" – even if you fell over a bunch of clowns. It's not a good starting point. You could try some more obvious openers such as how do you know (insert host's name). If the guy answers with *"we met at a wife swapping party in 1972"*, arrange a date immediately. If he says we met at a book club then keep going as you may eventually dig deep enough to find something communal, or something you can both be amused by. Unless he's reading Dostoevsky.

Conversation is just about being interesting and being interested. As long as you remember it's a two-way thing. Be curious. Ask questions and listen to the answers. Make comments. It may sound easy but as you know some people really don't do this well at all. There are those who think conversation is all about talking about themselves. These people are sometimes called men. However, keep listening and look like you care about the answers. Hopefully you are up on current affairs, so you have stuff to talk about if anything topical crops up. If someone mentions something they are interested in i.e. history, and you have something interesting to add then go ahead. And really don't introduce into the conversation dull stuff about yourself. Not everyone wants to hear about your children, dogs, or pet gerbil. And keep focused even if you do catch the eye of the good-looking guy in the corner. Stay present with attention focused on the person you are talking to, and with a bit of luck Mr Goodlooking might just be their single brother. Equally it may be their husband.

There is an obvious commonality of two strangers meeting at an event. It is that both of you have been invited. If you establish that initially it could lead onto more interesting conversation.

If the chat starts to falter don't start looking over their shoulder and then making feeble excuses about needing to go to the bathroom. You've only been there five minutes? Instead pull someone nearby into the conversation. Or down your glass quickly and suggest you go find another drink – together. That gets you into other people's orbits without being rude to the person you're talking to. Alternatively you might overhear a conversation and steer yourself into joining with "I couldn't help overhearing what you just said and I wanted to say etc". Why not? You're at a party and the concept of which is to have fun and meet people.

Questions are conversation fuel and who knows you might just learn something as well. So go ahead and ask. Perhaps because I'm a journalist I always want to know more - but then so should you. Steer clear of being personal, but asking questions and showing interest is something you can do naturally that will really help you meet people. And it's enjoyable. All you need to do is remember EVERYONE has something interesting to say, and more so if it's a subject they are passionate about it. (Having said that there are people who might have seen a Martian walking down the road this morning and still make it sound dull). You might have to initially pretend you like model making, trainspotting or whatever, but it could just be the starting point for something that engages you more. I know someone who is an ace at pretending he likes football. In truth he hates it, but he enjoys challenging himself when in the back of a black cab. If the taxi driver starts talking about last night's football match this particular passenger will take part in the conversation as though they were at the event. He just keeps agreeing and throwing in generic comments like "did you see that goal" (then crosses your fingers and hopes there was one). You can just go with the flow and try feeding back what you hear. You never know when someone you are talking to may have other interests that are more aligned with yours or they might know someone else who does and introduce you.

The most important point is to be positive. It is such an attractive trait. Laugh at a joke. Smile at someone's efforts. Be appreciative of your environment. Your host has gone to some lengths to get you all together and when your host was making plans for a party you were in her/his thoughts. That's nice to know isn't it? You got a chance to go out, meet people and even if you didn't meet the man of your dreams you got to practice your conversational skills and experience being around people. Did you get any contact details? Did you expand your network? Keep turning up and at some point, somehow you will find your way to the person you want to meet. Meet one to meet THE one.

Before you and I leave the party, grab our coats, shove a cocktail sausage and a mini burger in our handbags, here's a good tip on how to proactively swap contact details? It used to be that you'd flirt your socks off and wait to be asked for your phone number. Or you'd ask for theirs. Which often felt like trying to cross a busy motorway with your eyes shut. None of that is necessary anymore. Most people can be found from their name and area of business by going via either Facebook or Linkedin. You make contact then when accepted you can direct message. But how do you ensure that making contact is welcome? How do you steer a conversation so it leads to a date? It goes like this……

So, there you are, sipping and dipping when you suddenly find yourself in a conversation with someone you are attracted to. Let's say you both really enjoy history. Don't forget to listen before you indulge your own passion for the Tudors, WW1 or

*Delissa Needham*

the Tolpuddle Martyrs. All conversation is two way. Now grab that passion for a communal subject and use it as fuel towards securing a meeting again in the future. Be proactive and say how much you enjoyed that chat. If you can, mention historical lectures you attend and gauge the reaction. You are not suggesting at this stage that they join you but just highlighting that's what you do. Provided you have their name and occupation you can move on to talk to someone else. When you make contact via social media you can say I enjoyed talking to you and by the way there's a history event (lecture) next week, I have a spare ticket. Would you like to join me? It's the simplest, least embarrassing way to proactively secure a date from a first-time meeting with someone. This method works across all hobbies and passions - even trainspotting.

Chapter Thirteen

# HOW TO GET IN THE RIGHT ROOM.

A focussed strategy will help you be proactive and encourage you to examine what it is you want from a relationship. No bad thing when you look at the divorce statistics out there. Perhaps if we were all as clear about what we wanted from relationships as we are about our cleaning products, life would be simpler.

You've basically got three ways to meet a new man – four if you don't mind wearing a sandwich board.

Your choices are….

1. Online dating
2. Introduction agencies
3. Go out.

Yes – just go out. Options 1 & 2 aren't my cup of tea and are the very reasons for writing this book. Option 3 is fun. It works just by being more focussed on where you go and what you do. Do your research. At worst you'll have a good time. Remember you can say hello to anyone, you can smile at anyone, and you can always have a fun conversation with a complete stranger. Life is too short not to.

Going out has its disappointments just like online dating and introduction agencies, but at the very least you will meet new people and widen your network, and therefore your chances of meeting someone. It's important to remind yourself that somewhere a single man is looking and so are you. You just need to get in the same 'room'.

So where? Where do you go?

Obviously, you want to go to places and events where you are most likely to meet the right man for you. Where are you most likely to have success.

First decide who you are looking for. Be clear to yourself who that person is. If you can identify what you most want in a man, then you can work out who they might be, and therefore where they could be. Apply some obvious logic to what you want and then when you head off out for the evening you've already upped your chance of success.

If you're certain that you need to meet a man with intelligence, then you need to be socialising where intelligent people congregate. It's that basic. If you want a man who looks after his teeth and has a nice smile, then go to a dentist seminar. Seriously. There is one every year in Olympia or Earls Court and another even bigger one in Birmingham. It will be rammed full of men with nice teeth. There are 12,000 male dentists in the UK and they can't all be married, ancient or gay.

So, what is important to you in a person you spend time with.

If it matters that the man in your life is as dotty about dogs as you are then you are <u>less</u> likely to find your man on the golf course. Why not? Because if you've got a dog and you care for it, you walk it. You don't walk a dog at golf. It's a single man you want so there's no wife to walk the dog. How many hours in the day does a man have available to walk? I'm not saying your man isn't one who enjoys golf but do ask yourself - when is he going to find the time? If you want to meet a man who likes the outdoors, team sports, leisure pursuits like sailing, windsurfing, rugby etc then don't expect to splash past him while he's doing 20 lengths at the local swimming pool. He doesn't have the time. Its basic logic.

You've decided you want to meet someone so now decide what specifics you are immoveable on and let that one thing signpost the direction of where you go to find that person. There are things you know you can't change in someone i.e cleanliness is teachable, intelligence isn't. If you know you could never fancy a man with a low IQ then focus on finding someone with intelligence. Maybe you are immoveable on religion or possibly financial parity is important to you. Stick to the specifics that are unchangeable like a sense of humour. Anything else you can change – fitness, health, weight, etc. Yes, it is possible to lead a man away from the takeaway queue.

Really it is. You might find that he clings like a sobbing limpet to the edge of the bar if you try and prise him from a pint but when a man is in love with a woman, he usually wants to please. If that means taking more care of his health and weight, then that's terrific. Everyone's a winner.

To imagine the kind of person you are going to meet is also to envisage success. I'm not saying don't be open to love wherever it may come from, but if you start with an idea of what matters to you then at least you can set off, and in the right direction. If you get distracted on route by an unlikely man, then hey that's the serendipity of love. But start with focus and it will help move you forward. You wouldn't get in your car and set off to a new location without first checking the roadmap. You won't be heading out to unlikely places but hopefully going to more likely ones. Look at it this way. If you want to eat fish for supper you don't go to the butchers. Tea and biscuits are in the same location in the supermarket, butter and toilet paper are not in the same place (except in *Last Tango in Paris*). There are 20 different shopping aisles and you instinctively and logically know where most things are. So now apply the same instinct and logic to your wanting to meet a man. Start with what you are looking for and then focus on where you can find it.

Once you understand the who then you'll be able to work out the where. What are this person's circumstances likely to be? Why is he looking for someone? Think about what they are likely to want. This is the way to lift the rug in the right place.

The 'where' is often common sense. Just think about what people really do and why. Think it through.

I mentioned a client in a previous chapter who was socially busy – all the time. She played bridge on Mondays, sang in the choir on Tuesdays and played tennis on Wednesdays and never met a man. My client told me she wanted to meet a 'well educated', intelligent man who was her "social equal". That's a narrow-minded way of looking at a potential relationship in my view but she'd decided that's what mattered to her. So, we suggested she swap one of her activity nights for a game of chess instead. Chess requires strategic thinking and a brain, but it's also been taught to boys in public schools, so there was an increased chance of meeting the kind of man she was looking for. We researched the chess club in her town, and it definitely ticked her boxes. But she wouldn't be persuaded. She preferred to stick to bridge. Shame. Lots of single ladies in the bridge club.

While forming a profile in your mind of your likely kind of man, you should also consider what his relationship objectives are likely to be. This will help you not to waste time and to avoid disappointment. About the time that the Candace Bushnell wrote her book 'Sex in the City' and created a storm, it was joked that New York women had a check list when dating men. It went something like – what are your career prospects, what property do you own, are you paying alimony, do you want children etc. This side of the pond we just want to have fun but it's not a bad idea to decide what matters to you and where a man fits into that. His relationship objectives are of course likely to be age related. So be clear to yourself about what you want, figure out what he is likely or will want, and you will save time and disappointment

1. If the man for you is aged 30-35 then you are looking in the marrying group. It's a limited period of well stacked shelves so don't waste it. What do you want? If it's to get married, then don't waste your time with someone who doesn't see you that way? Move on. I know a woman who said to her date on their third outing *"I want to get married and have children so if that's not what you want then let's stop this now"*. I know she said that because the anecdote was repeated by the groom at their wedding. So focus. It's all too easy to be distracted by a hope for a future with someone that realistically isn't going to happen.

2. If your ideal man is in the 35-40 age group, then this is not far off the peak divorce rate. So the men you will meet in this age group are a) still looking for the right woman, b) keen to stay a bachelor or c) recently divorced. This last group either likes being married or is not in a rush to do that again. Which are you dating? If you are not dating anyone then you need to get out there. The shelves are emptying. Get meeting new people and potential partners.

3. The age group of people in their 40's to 50's has less availability, but you are at least looking in the peak divorce rate group. So, while you may be looking for your second marriage, so are many men. Many who get divorced get remarried. Timing though is crucial. Be careful that you are not the catalyst for the divorce. Not a nice situation to be in and not least because 'catalysts' don't usually make it

over the line to be the next wife. There's too much difficulty to get through first.

4. The 50-60 age group is when the divorce rate is high but it's dropping off peak. There are perpetual bachelors in this category, and they usually want to stay that way. It takes a lot to change their thinking. Some single men in this group will have decided they are now looking for someone to have children with. Most women in this age group are menopausal so the most potential man in the 50-60 age group is a divorcee with children.

5. And then there's the 60-70 age group. Surprisingly the number of brides and grooms aged 65 and over went up by 46% in a decade, going from 7,468 in 2004 to 10,937 in 2014. And it's still going up.

So hurrah for an encouraging statistic.

In this age group there are single men who want to meet a lovely woman (could be you) as a partner to enjoy shared experiences with until someone nails down the coffin.

So let's come back to thinking about the 'where'. Where are you most likely to find what you are looking for? If you think a little deeper about the circumstances and the likely emotions of the available singles in this group, you will begin to understand more about the 'why' and the 'who' and that will enable you to apply some common sense knowledge to the 'where'.

To explain what I mean let's take as an example from this 60+ age group and apply some realistic thinking.

This age group finds it hardest to meet single women and most often rely on their network of friends. Hence you need to get out there and meet people. Available men in this group will either be a bachelor, a divorcee, or a widower. There's also the married man looking for an affair, but if this appeals to you then put down my book, find the nearest biscuit tin lid and hit yourself over the head with it three times.

The widower is the most likely for a long-term relationship. Why not the other two? Well if you really feel like cracking the hard nut that is a 60+ bachelor then be my guest. The divorcee is either feeling a little burnt, or now looking just for sexual fun before settling down again. Do you want to be on his list? So, let's look at the widower.

All my male widower friends in that age group have similar specific habits, character traits, values, activities etc. There are many things they all have in common, and one in particular. They like being married.

I can't imagine how awful it must be to have loved and shared your life with someone whom you have adored, who has been your partner, your other half, your reason to be for many years, for possibly decades – and for that person to have died. It must feel lonely, and the future must at times seem so bleak. To wake in the early hours of the morning feeling alone. The grief that turns into brief moments of anger at being left. The sense of enormous loss with every struggle and every joy to be encountered alone. A widower has lost someone they love, and they miss that person. Of course it takes time – years but often the desire not to feel lonely anymore fuels the desire to meet someone. But they don't know how. My single widowed male friends of this age would rather not try than fail. So they stay where it's comfortable and that feeling guides where they look. It may well be years since the 'widower' went on a date, it's a scary proposition. The only person who would understand how he feels is no longer there to help. Online dating doesn't work for the widower any more than it works for you. Strangers in a strange land is too much. You won't find them on dating sites and if you did, you'd probably pass them by no matter how lovely, kind, funny, generous, intelligent they are, because online sites just don't convey all that.

All my male widower friends married in their 30's and their children have their own lives and no longer live at home. The deceased wife always did the cooking for the family except for usually the one annual occasion when father/husband cooked his speciality. Someone has always taken care of him while he earns the money. So he doesn't know how to cook but he is learning. This is his age group and its traditionally how couples operate in relationships. Now he's the one in the supermarket looking confused over a pack of mince. The man who has a trolley filled with the same basic things he can handle - meat, fish, wine, and muesli. Some widowers I know had shared interests and activities with their wives like football, cycling, walking the dog, reading books. Other widower friends shared sports with their wives. They played tennis, went sailing, skiing etc but as their sporting friends are all married, they now do activities that don't need partners like golf. Those that played tennis as a couple don't play tennis now. They all still work. It keeps them connected and sane. If they're not entrepreneurs then they work 9-5, catch trains and shop in supermarkets in the evening on the way home or stock up at weekends. In looking for a partner, every single one of my male widower friends in the 60+ years plays safe. Often, they have a busy social life and rely on friends when it comes to meeting a suitable single woman. They rarely look beyond the office or their immediate circle. Lazy? Scared? Or both? I don't know. And yet they want to be married, they like to love and be loved and are ready to love again. They don't want to be alone. They are just like you. It is likely they have the same hopes for a shared future.

You've just got to get in the same room.

- What are you looking for?
- What is the one thing that matters to you?
- What kind of person fits that brief?
- Who are they likely to be and what do they want?
- Where are they? Where is the playground?

## Chapter Fourteen

# RESEARCH IS YOUR BEST DATING FRIEND.

Let's say you have realised you are seeking an intelligent single man, 60+, a widower.

The world of events is loaded with things for intelligent folk to do from debates, to talks, lectures, political meetings etc. Go find.

The 'go out' approach involves deciding on the kind of man you want to meet and filling your diary with focussed social engagements and events where you are most likely to meet that person. Where are you most likely to be successful - and where you are likely to enjoy yourself. This is all meant to be fun. Make it so.

How do you fill your social diary with events where you are likely to be successful? By doing your research or paying a researcher to do it for you if you've got the budget. It can take time for researchers to find enough events to cover a month or more of activities but once you've got going, you'll know what works and what doesn't. Then you keep going in the direction that does work. What can you work out about 60+ single male widowers? He's not sitting on his own at the bar of an expensive club in London because he's never been a member of such a club, and he won't start now. Single widowed men also don't usually prop up the bar in the gastro pub. Most of my widowed 60+ male friends congregate regularly in one place. Whether they earn a living running a hedge fund or by plumbing in your washing machine men from all walks of life meet and enjoy male company in the pub. It's a great leveller – in the pub everyone has something to contribute to the conversation. The grittier the pub the better. Women are happiest somewhere special with a glass of prosecco, men are at their most comfortable anywhere serving great beer, cheap cheese rolls, pork scratchings and pickled eggs. Call it a generalisation if you like but drop into any pub late Saturday morning anywhere in the country and you'll see workman's boots and overalls mixing with leather deck shoes and well ironed jeans. Enter at your peril but whatever you do don't frighten the horses.

If top of your list is that you want to meet a man with a great brain, then most towns and cities are rich with likely events. If you are lucky enough to be in London, then events to look out for are does wine lunches. Or go to some of the lunches where history authors are speaking. Go to some book launches. Once you start to look you will see there is plenty going on – you are looking for events where there is time and opportunity to mingle with other guests. If you live in the country, then do your research in the nearest town. Get off your bum and get out – or start knitting your long johns now because your old age is going to be cold and lonely.

What do the 60+ widowers who are like my male friends enjoy? What interests them. How do they spend their leisure time? Of course, there are sports like golf, shooting, riding, sailing. rugby, football, rowing etc. Which of those can you access and, importantly, enjoy. It's my number one rule that you enjoy the activity or event first and foremost and that you attend with the prime purpose of doing that, and hopefully meeting many new people. You must get out of your comfort zone and stop worrying about how you might feel. Just do it. What about politics? If you need to meet a man whose political thinking matches yours then join your local political party and volunteer to help with campaigning.

60+ is an age group of intelligent people who read and enjoy history and have done since school. When I was working at the History Channel the greater part of the audience was in this group. So research history lectures have a look at book festivals where favourite history authors speak. You could even think about attending history re-enactments. Go to any WW2 lecture and you'll find a wealth of Antony Beever readers. A friend of mine was a head of fundraising at a charity until she retired in her early sixties. She took a part-time volunteer job as a guide at the cathedral in her town. She was showing people around the cathedral on tours and one day the right person was on her tour. It happens. So what can you do?

Where can you go and where can you be involved in the likely area where you could also meet someone who is right for you. Your first step is to think about and research the most likely playgrounds that fit the profile of your type of man.

This is how it worked for Leona who became a client just before her 60th birthday. She and her husband had divorced 5 years ago, and Leona hadn't met anyone new. She hated the whole online dating thing and tried an introduction agency, but it was costly and unsuccessful. Leona was determined to meet someone so to start with she'd joined an expensive members-only club and unfortunately met plenty of women like herself. She'd gone on singles holidays and met plenty of women like herself. She'd learnt to play bridge and met plenty of women like herself. She'd joined the local golf club and met plenty of women like herself. She'd gone on a wine tasting course and met women like herself. Ditto learning a foreign language.

She told us what kind of man she was looking for and then we drilled a bit further and found out in more detail what kind of man she was really looking for. What really mattered to her. He would be a conservative voter, an entrepreneur, a fit man, a healthy man, an intelligent man. A dog lover. The Dateist researchers were busy for nearly two weeks, but Leona eventually ended up operating a very busy but very targeted calendar of events. It took several social engagements, many disappointments and hopeful but wrong situations, lots of trying this and that etc, but eventually Leona was in the right place at the right time and met someone at a vintage car rally.

She googled the detail on the classic car he was exhibiting and then went over to say hello to his soppy dog.

So, to summarise this chapter – know what you are looking for, apply some logic, then plan and research accordingly.

I hugely admire my clients who have decided to find new love. It takes courage. Knowing you want to share your life with someone but knowing right now that such a person is likely to be a stranger to you. But if you are determined to be successful, you work at it and you apply some logical thinking then you will achieve your goal.

*Chapter Fifteen*

# USING THE INTERNET FOR DATING.

It may seem a little strange for me to talk about dating using the internet. I'm not a big fan. If you think returning Amazon parcels is disheartening – then you've not experienced online dating. I prefer to encourage and help people to meet in the real world, however I can't ignore what is an important and a widely used way of meeting new partners And there are times when it's wonderfully successful.

It is a useful dating tool, but you know when you order an online delivery from your supermarket you don't choose the apples that end up in your basket. You don't look at them, touch, smell or feel them. So if someone else - and in online dating that 'someone' else is an algorithm - chooses for you a 'pappy' apple with zilch flavour and no sweetness then you only have yourself to blame. Get off your bum and go pick your own apple. That's my view on it. My main concern is that love is blind - or in this case the need for love makes us blind.

*How I Met My Man and How You Can Meet Yours*

When you want something so much you believe too easily, fantasise too easily, and buy into a dream all too quickly. Caution and normal wary responses are thrown aside because you want this to work. If you meet someone by expanding your network, then there is always a connection. Complete strangers you meet on the internet can be anyone, of course - and there are no social restraints on their behaviour. No consequences. Having said that, I acknowledge that online dating has been revolutionary and particularly for women. Remember that horrible expression, *'she's on the shelf'*. It meant you were done for on the marriage market – doomed to a life of spinsterhood. Condemned. It's an expression that effectively turned women over 40 into the equivalent of a pot of unwanted jam. Their status reduced to that of out-of-date confiture. Even the label 'spinster' is ageing. It sounds sort of pointy and sharp whereas bachelor sounds like fun. Especially 'distinguished bachelor'. Older women don't get held in similar esteem but online dating has been very empowering for single women. Whether you are 30 years old or 70 years old there are now many opportunities to meet someone and marry. There is a huge number of singles in the older age groups who sign up to dating agencies and a huge number who meet the right man and get married. This deliberate way of meeting someone was once considered the last resort but now its first choice.

So whereas the widows of yesterday's world were unlikely to marry again, now they do. I've met many couples who have met through online dating. It does work. So that's the good news.

Now the bad news.

The bad news is that it's a cesspit of deceit and self-delusion. Firstly, you will come across a lot of people telling lies about their age. Why does someone lie about their age when you can usually find out the truth in a one click. A client who has been slowly getting to know a girl, has been lying about his age by a good ten years. But the girl in question only had to do minimal research, particularly in business areas, and there is his age. Not a good start for a relationship. Unfortunately, people will also lie about their looks (using a much younger photograph), and about their intentions, or their single status. Sometimes exaggerating the truth or hiding it.

Yes, there's plenty of fish in the sea but you are about to discover you must wade through a lot of plastic before you catch a mackerel. You will quickly learn to be adept at spotting anything suspicious. There are some dating websites with software that screens messages for inappropriate sexual content. Red flags are raised when a guy signs up and contacts a lot of women in different age groups. So do your research on which on-line sites are careful about how their members interact and what their intentions are. I've heard a ton of horror stories, but equally several success stories. You will eventually meet someone so don't give up hope.

So where do you start? You can choose some of the bigger sites like eHarmony or Match.com or you can be a little bit more specialised. There are a variety of sites depending on whether you want one that specialises in farmers, medics, vicars, rugby players, knitters, etc.

By now you should have created your man's profile from your specifications.

So now take that profile and think about which type of site that man is likely to be on. Is it Telegraph dating, or Guardian dating? Are you looking for a type of profession? Or a particular religion?

There are websites for pet lovers, websites for country lovers, websites for town lovers etc. Even ones specifically aimed at dating fishermen. Although dating an angler seems a bit unpromising to us. Every fisherman I've ever seen is out at the crack of dawn putting wiggly worms onto hooks and sitting by a river listening to the test match. What would they want a partner for? To put the ham in the ham sandwich? I'm not saying fishermen aren't passionate but if you are looking for someone to throw you over the kitchen table a man with the patience to sit for hours by a riverbank waiting for a carp to show up is probably not it. You'd be much better off with a rugby player. 15 beefy broken nose players to choose from? What's not to like?

Dating online is a scary and daunting process and often disappointing but a good starting point is to find a site that suits you. Perhaps you would like someone with particular religious beliefs for example the Jewish religion. There's a good online dating site called JWed: https://www.jwed.com/.

They've succeeded in helping 3,500 marriages and while it's difficult to have a sense of who is marriage minded and who isn't, this number of marriages is proof that the site has a good intent. You can't lose by just giving it a go.

The fact that internet dating has grown exponentially shows that it has a role to play. As I said above, it has been especially empowering for women. I am not anti-dating via the internet, but I see it as only one tool in your toolkit. It's a lot more fun going out and about. Social interaction is necessary for our wellbeing. The many things that attract us to each other can't be pixelated. How many times have you bought something online only to try it on and realise it is completely unsuitable? The cut, the feel, the smell - what looks great on the page may not, in reality, be for you. It's the same with dating. A chance glance in a shop and you may see something attractive hanging up in a store, maybe the buttons, the drape, the sheen caught your attention. Whatever it is, you were out there, and you found it. You were out there.

The lockdowns certainly made singles realise how much they miss having someone to share their life with. Not necessarily for love or sex but someone to go out to dinner with, to go to the movies with, to share hobbies and passions with. The number of people who joined online dating sites during lockdown increased by an average of over 40%. Interesting considering they couldn't physically date, but many daters used the lockdown to get to know people on-line – enjoy some conversations and build some relationships. Then they arranged to meet once the lockdown was lifted.

Very often those specifications that every hopeful dater aims to fill, goes in the wastepaper basket not long after they've met someone. People who get to know each other online over a period of time, and then meet may be initially disappointed but very often quickly accept that although the person doesn't fit the initial brief, they still like them. The intense relationship built up over time online can override any shortcomings in that list of specific characteristics.

Also I often hear internet dating stories that mirror my own experience. The one person I met and connected with, was someone I already knew. In fact he lived in my street. We had met through a mutual friend and even dated a few times. This is not unusual. Only recently a friend who was on a dating site reconnected with someone from her past. It happens more often than you would think.

The important thing to remember about online dating is that it all begins with a photograph. And photos as we all know aren't really an indication of someone's personality. There are websites where members can conceal their photos and only reveal themselves to other members when they choose to. This means that people are less visually driven but unfortunately this system also backfires because 82% of members will ignore profiles that don't come with a photograph. So writing a good profile becomes even more essential as an indicator of character. So try to write something that really says something about you and who you are. Try to show personality and humour.

I'm not against dating websites but my reason for writing this book is to show you that there is another way. It's the one I personally prefer. I don't use dating sites because I consider them unromantic so definitely don't let that stop you using them. It's not a method that works for me because I have never fancied a man for his looks. Mostly I like men with not much hair but there are men with not much hair who are very sexy and some men who are not. And you won't get the difference from a photo.

There is something else. You must keep your wits about you. Here is a very loud 'BEWARE'. I reiterate that online dating can be a useful tool and I know many lovely stories of women who have used it successfully - but I also know of some horror stories. My advice is don't trust until proven otherwise. Dating in the offline world is a place where it's easier to find out more about someone. Online you are more vulnerable. You probably feel vulnerable enough at the start of the process and that in itself makes you a target. (Look up catfishing online and find out more). Beware being asked for naked photos. It makes you vulnerable to blackmail. Don't be fooled by sad stories from a stranger. He's probably telling the same story to several other women. Don't part with money AT ALL. Not even to send an iPhone voucher. Don't give out information about yourself i.e date of birth. And if you do go on a date with the stranger, you met online do be aware of the message you are giving out with your appearance. Leave the expensive jewellery and designer handbag at home unless you are sure of the person you are meeting. Look immaculate but don't look like the rich widow/rich divorcee etc.

In summary - please be aware that there are men online who upload fake photos and fake profiles - i.e. who doesn't trust a doctor? These are fake 'available' men who earn a good living from conning vulnerable women out of money. You may think that's not you - but you don't know the level of scams being used. So I say again - don't trust until proven otherwise and, you are sure.

And above all - do your background research. Find out as much as possible about the person you are connecting to. If they're a real doctor, then they have a medical registration. Does the information you are given add up? The warnings I'm giving above are based on the following true story. One of many true stories.

Lydia was happily married (she thought) and had been for 25 years. She had lovely children, now young adults, and she and her husband had plans for retirement. Then lockdown happened:

## Lydia

My husband had always travelled for work. As we had young children it made sense for me to stop and look after the home. It worked well I thought until lockdown meant that he was at home - a lot. It became apparent that something was awry and after a confrontation he admitted to having affairs, some with much younger women. We were divorced whilst living in the same house during lockdown which brought its own pressures. However I survived, he moved out to be with a much younger partner and I was alone. It was still difficult to go out, so I turned to the internet. Soon I was exchanging messages with interested parties. It was exciting, no longer spending the evenings binge watching a series. One man who got in touch was a doctor, working in very remote areas and so it was difficult to communicate regularly, but when we did connect it was great. He was interested in every aspect of my life; every detail and he told me about his 12-year-old son and the dangers of his job. How lucky he was to have this opportunity. Being new to the dating game and having a 25-year relationship in fragments, I loved the attention. Yes, it was intense, but I felt great that someone felt strongly about me when we hadn't even met. Some weeks into the chats he asked me for a naughty picture. I was a little taken aback. It's not something I'd ever done. I didn't know him. He laughed and made some comment about trying new things. The conversation moved on. I was too uneasy about it. Thank goodness for my prudish stance it later transpired. Some weeks later I had a phone call from him. He was upset about his son. He needed an iTunes voucher so he could play games with his friends. He was working in a remote area saving lives and couldn't access his bank to get one organised. Could I possibly help? 30 pounds should do it. Well, I felt for the guy, so I sent 50. It was the least I could do for a doctor. He thanked me profusely when he was next able to get in touch. I was happy to help. I felt we bonded. We both loved helping people. Me as a teacher, him as a doctor. Then he phoned in great agitation. His son was sick. It was going to cost $25,000 to get him an operation abroad. He had $15,000, but time was of the essence. Could I help? As I was still going through my divorce, I couldn't give away £10,000 without having to show the lawyers which I didn't want to do. I was so sorry not to be able to help financially. He understood but was distracted during our conversations. Many heavy sighs. It was really worrying him. I heard from him less. He explained that he was focussing on his son and raising money to help him. I missed him, our chats, our bond. He kept me informed as to how much money he needed, only five thousand to go, only three. How generous people were being. I so wanted to be part of this positivity. Helping a 12-year-old to get better. Who wouldn't do that? Still my hands were tied. It wasn't until I was out walking with a friend that I came to understand what was really going on. She, quite rightly, asked me how well I really knew this guy. Had we ever Skyped, met on Zoom or Face Time? No we hadn't, but he had sent lovely videos of where he was and what he was doing, but he was behind the camera at all times. He blamed his uselessness with technology as to why I couldn't see his face. I could relate as I'm a bit the same.

Then my friend asked what I could find out about him. Surely there must be some imprint out there in the ether somewhere. So the next time I was home alone, rather than go to my favourite dating sights I started to look for him. Facebook, Instagram, military records, doctors' registrations. What did I find? Nothing, zilch. Nor for his son. Now, by this time I have alarm bells going off in my head. I know that reading this you probably have your head in your hands wondering how I could've possibly been this stupid, but it sounded so plausible at the time. Plus I was emotionally engaged. The next step was to google iTunes scams. Well that really opened my eyes. This is big business. Shortly afterwards I blocked, deleted, and removed every contact. I may try again in the future, but I need to be a lot more wary and savvier than I have been and put safeguards in place.

It is possible to find love in the digital space, but just keep your eyes open. In a way you are just another 'tourist' being ripped off in a strange city.

Social media can also be useful but again tread wary. If you use Facebook, then how about a 'Retread'?

Have you ever trawled through Facebook looking for ex boyfriends? Or Google even. Give it a go – it's good fun if nothing else. Ever wondered what happened to such and such?

When two people have known each other in the past as friends, school mates etc, there is often the foundations for a new relationship. Common ground is a good starting point, and again it expands your own network. You never know who may have been holding a candle to your memory.

Facebook is a good tool for marketing. So market yourself. Take control of your own PR. But be aware of stranger danger at all times i.e no house details, no travel plans, no obvious wealth on display. Keep your private settings high.

*How I Met My Man and How You Can Meet Yours*

You can also use Facebook to join groups. Chess groups, re-enactment groups, political groups, discussion groups, dog owners' groups etc. Use the internet to gather information about events near you. You are a real person so go to real events. Why would you prefer to stare at a screen?

# PART 4:
# THINK YES!

*Chapter Sixteen*

## **KNOCK OFF THE CORNERS.**

Here's betting that the list you are clutching specifying your ideal man, will not have a single negative thing on it.

What woman ever says – I don't mind if he's a lump of lard. Or pass me the bald headed, nose picker – he's my man. Yeh – I'm at the front of the queue for the farter with the beer gut and arse spilling over his jeans. Gimme, Gimme, Gimmee!!!

NOOOOOO!!! No gal is looking for one of those. Everyone wants the same thing. He's got to look like Tom Cruise, Matthew McConaughey, Omar Sy etc. He's got to be fit. He's got to be healthy. He's got to be intelligent. He's got to have money. He's got to be tall. He's got to have nice eyes.

He's got to be from Planet Zog! Might as well be with the miniscule chance you have of actually finding him.

I mean really – it's like you never went into the butcher's shop to buy steak and came out with pork sausages.

*How I Met My Man and How You Can Meet Yours*

Ladies – you are looking for the impossible. What you want is as rare as the proverbial rocking horse doo doo.

You gotta work with what there is. Change your thinking. Change your man. What you want is out there, but right now it's wearing different wrapping.

Take our friend Lucy for instance. When she first met Colin, he weighed in at a hefty 18 stone. Colin thought a six pack was what you kept in the fridge in the drinks compartment.

Six months after meeting Lucy – he was a fit and healthy 14 stone with muscle and a sexual appetite like a tiger.

Lucy went to work. First there was the visit to the nutritionist, then there was the motivation. Attractive slim Lucy was one helluva motivation. Lucy was shaking her ass, not wagging her finger.

It boiled down to Lucy or buns.

**Colin chose Lucy.**

It's amazing what a determined woman can do. Colin dressed better. He ate healthier. He was happier.

So much happier.

The only peeps losing out was the local baker.

Underneath all that excess fat was a fit healthy sexy man waiting to get out. And Lucy knew just how to make it happen. She fell in love with the guy at first sight but being a fit healthy

162

woman it just was not in her thinking to date a man who was also not fit and healthy. So, it was either bring him round to her way of thinking or the relationship (particularly the sex) just wouldn't get off the starting line.

Human beings are all very different – it's what makes love work. But if it doesn't tick your box – if something doesn't spark then it never will, but don't overlook anyone because they don't conform to your rigid list. We women are very good at changing men. It's what we do.

John Preston's recent book on Maxwell tells an interesting story about the first few days of the media mogul's marriage. A few days into being a husband he wrote a letter to his wife in which he specified the 6 most important rules for a happy marriage. One of those rules was to advise his new wife not to nag.

What?

Ask a woman not to nag?

It would be easier to explain where Whitstable is to a mackerel.

We nag. It's in our DNA. We learn it from our mother and so on.

Use that skill to change what you have into what you want. When you meet a man and you like him, but he doesn't fit your specifications, then change him. And if you must nag then so be it, just don't overdo it and make sure there's a carrot to entice progress.

*How I Met My Man and How You Can Meet Yours*

Women are naturally clever at getting what they want without confrontation. Women always aim to win the war – we don't bother with the skirmish. We know how to motivate. And we are clever at turning things in our favour while making men think it's their idea.

So don't just automatically turn away because what you are looking at doesn't fit your strict list of wants. Some things are changeable. He might just need the right motivation. Could you be that motivation?

Here's a story of two people meeting who really couldn't be more chalk and cheese. There was a lot of spark between these two people but some issues needed fixing before this love affair could take off. But then it was my friend Joanie who was fixing things. Not much stands in her way. Joanie knew very decisively that she had met her ideal man. But there was a problem. Not an insurmountable one but it was unpleasant. It would take some fortitude to fix it.

## Joanie 38

I had been single for a good few years, ever since my husband left me for a woman younger than my daughter. I've shied away from a new relationship. I'd sort of tried but I felt I was meeting more men who were like my husband. City types. Men in suits with big money goals. I wanted someone with more caring goals in life. Someone who thought about the environment - about the world around us and our place in it. But most of all I didn't want to be hurt again. I know it's a big generalisation about the city men I'm describing but that was all I was meeting. All my friends were in that circle and so I was just meeting what I already knew all too well. Eventually I moved out of London to a house in the country where I had a few friends and family nearby. I was happier that way. And the more I thought about it, what would a partner and a new relationship really bring me? More pain but then I didn't want to be single all my life. I did think it would be nice to meet someone to be with. Someone who shared my interests in the environment and who cared about the future of the planet. An intelligent man who unlike my ex-husband wasn't just money motivated. But the chances of that happening were slim. I wasn't looking so how did I think it was going to happen? And then I met Steve.

Not long after moving into my new house, the toilet got blocked. Unfortunately this was no ordinary blockage - it was way down in the sewage pipe and the backlog meant the problem was now appearing in the backyard. It was horribly messy.

So I called a local drainage company.

Steve was the emergency drainage expert that arrived to solve the problem.

If anyone had said to me, where do you think you might meet the big love of your life, I would not have said hosing poop off my patio. I offered him a coffee and had to stand well back when I handed it to him. He was a big ball of hair. Scruffy wild hair and shaggy beard in a ginger colour. There were bits of

*How I Met My Man and How You Can Meet Yours*

toast crumbs from his breakfast still in his beard. And he really didn't smell nice. A cross between something whiffy and something very disinfectanty. Ugh. I handed him his coffee. He was tall and very softly spoken and leaning over the stable door of my kitchen back garden he started to talk to me about drains, sewage systems, the environment generally. He was so intelligent. He was kind, practical and considerate. A nice man. A fascinating man. He was an environmentally aware man. He talked about how he was trying to be self-sufficient with his allotment and the plants he was growing in his back garden using natural methods of fertilisation. He was composting most of his rubbish. Sure he smelt toxic, but he was greener than green, and I really liked that about him.

And he had these piercing blue eyes, and a lovely smile in amongst all those whiskers.

Shame he stank. It was awful. You had to stand well back from the whiff of him. Pooooieeeee. I wondered what his wife or girlfriend thought of that! Then I realised I didn't want that picture. So I asked if the woman in his life minded what he did for a living. I was pleased to hear there wasn't a girlfriend. Not surprised either.

Steve collected his tools and left. He had to come back with a drain camera. I was quite glad he hadn't fixed it. And when he came back two days later, I made him another coffee and we had another chat. He was funny. He made me laugh. He played the piano and had a little boat in the nearby harbour he liked to sail at weekends. He was a peaceful sort of man.

*Delissa Needham*

I got to wondering if it was possible to change a smelly man. I guess you've got to really want to try. And I wanted to try. I liked him.

So two weeks later when the sewage pipe blocked again it wasn't such a bad thing. Yeh sure having poop popping up in your back garden and watching while the potential man of your dreams wades through your recent excrement is not an ideal start to a relationship. Certainly not what you'll see in a romcom on Netflix. Steve organised for a team to replace the faulty pipe, advised me on how to claim for it and then stood again by the backdoor accepting his tea from the ledge on the stable door, while I stood well back. How was I going to fix this?

But again we talked. A lovely conversation and then he asked me if I'd like to come and look at his boat at the weekend. I said yes - if you have a shower.

That was when the change first started.

I saw Steve the next weekend. He was showered and dressed nicely. Steve is a walking fountain of knowledge. Fascinating, energetic, enthusiastic. Interested in so many things. Over time the beard and the hair went and with a little encouragement from me he applied for a desk job. A senior role in his company so eventually he was office based and no longer physically on the job. He started studying at night and eventually moved into a completely different career. I also encouraged a complete change of diet, so he lost weight, dressed differently. He looks so completely different. You

167

*How I Met My Man and How You Can Meet Yours*

wouldn't recognise him as the same hairy smelly man leaning on my stable door. Eventually we moved in together. I sold my house, and we bought a new one and have been together for the last seven years.

They say you can't polish a turd. I did.

***

If you don't see what you want at first….take another look.

But sometimes there are things you really can't fix no matter how much you like someone.

Olivia tried to fix her man too but there were three of them in the relationship.

## Olivia 39

I spotted the presence of the third on our very first date. I should have walked away then.

During their first date, he drank a lot. Maybe he was nervous. When I said I needed to go home now, Brian offered to walk me. We had both finished our drinks and I wanted to go to the ladies before setting off for home. I was gone for 2, maybe 3 minutes. When I got back to the bar Brian had ordered another drink. A pint with a whiskey chaser and he was drinking both as fast as he could. It struck me as odd. Then I slowly realised over the next few dates that Brian had a drink problem. Although I liked him, I made the decision to throw the towel in. A drink problem needs to be dealt with otherwise there are three of you in the relationship and usually you are just a means to another drink. Until Brian could recognise he had a problem there would be no way forward. And he wasn't prepared to admit drink was an issue for him and seek the necessary help. So I decided this was not one for me and moved on. That took a lot of strength and foresight but eventually I met someone else. Brian went from bad to worse, eventually putting on weight and losing his job. The extent of his alcoholism became steadily more obvious to everyone but him. Sad but I know I made the right decision.

*Chapter Seventeen*

# THINK YOU WILL AND YOU WILL.

Just recently I advertised a carpet. A large wool one. Huge. It covered my living room floor. Brenda saw the ad and came to look at it, arriving in her estate car. She wanted the carpet for two young people who had just acquired a home but had no furnishings. A friend and I took up the carpet and rolled it. The process of rolling took two of us. I warned Brenda that it was too big for her car and that she'd need help to get it out of the house and onto a truck or something. But when Brenda arranged to collect it two days later, she turned up in her estate car, alone with no help. The carpet was twice the size of her car and heavy, but somehow, we got it in the back of her estate. I'm telling you this because the positive belief that it <u>was</u> possible is an incredible unstoppable energy. That was what made it possible.

Invariably the dating clients who really want a man do eventually get what they want. The time they devote to finding love eventually pays off. It has to. With all the single women in the world and all the single men in the world (no they don't all walk into Rik's bar), but they do get married. The statistics are wonderfully hopeful with many people getting married in all age brackets. Of course it's got to happen – eventually.

The single woman who is thinking positive is looking all the time. That's a key thing to do. Keep looking. This is the single woman who is expecting love to happen. Nothing gets past her. She is constantly filtering every man she meets. Measuring him against her tick box. A stranger stops to talk to her about her dog, or to ask for directions, or to open the door of the café and she is immediately sizing him up. That's a girl who gets what she wants. That's the girl who will meet a man. She is happy to chat to anyone because anyone can help her meet someone.

If you really want, you will get.

Think about what you want and think as well about what you need. Wouldn't that be better, instead of having a duplicate of your last boyfriend or trying to find a man that looks like Tom Cruise, George Clooney, Idris Elba (that holy ring of impossible 3 that you will NEVER find). How about giving a chance instead to someone whose company you enjoy? Someone you are relaxed with and have fun with. Someone who has the characteristics that you admire and value.

I don't advise that you choose according to the latest psychobabble which advises you to date someone who matches your family sibling position (first, second, or third child etc). This is such nonsense. Apparently middle children should never marry the oldest child. Older children who marry older children have a good marriage. This first born is listened to, treasured, and loved. Middle children are always fighting for attention against this older sibling – all the love goes to that older sibling who gets heard and seen and then the third sibling is born. The middle child is then undercut by the arrival of this younger child. And so the middle child learns the pain of being ignored and consequently wants to be heard. That middle child is likely to have big issues. Wanting to be seen and heard is the most obvious.

Whether any of that's true or not you have to ask yourself when you first meet a man and fall in love are really going to consider, or be bothered by knowing where he fits in the sibling line up? Of course not. You are in love. Nothing can go wrong, and you certainly are not going to walk away based on the hocus pocus of some psychological study. Can you imagine the scene? There you are sipping cocktails on a first date. You are with one of the holy trio (Clooney, Cruise or Elba) and you like him. Odd that. He is telling you about his many houses in many different continents and you project like you have a Hollywood director in your head. You are on the red carpet on Tom's/George's/Idris's arm. You are reclining on one of many continents, buying dresses on 5th avenue like Julia Roberts in Pretty Woman. And then you ask that million dollar make it or break it question. So, Tommykins, have you got any older or younger siblings? And you wait with bated breath and then comes the reply. He's a middle child. Whoosh!

The dream goes like a puff of smoke taking with it the chance to open a fridge door on any continent in the entire world. All because you won't date a middle child. Really?

Of course, the family is where character building happens, and this is bound to eventually have an impact on how a person conducts themselves in relationships and society. But it doesn't govern our instant reactions. It doesn't and shouldn't influence whether we like someone or not. However you might just let it inform you a little.

Meeting someone does of course get tougher the older you get. There's less around to like. Men, like women can go to seed. It's not called middle aged spread because it happens in your twenties. Eating for one can lead to lazy habits such as working all day at a desk and then ordering a pizza. Why not? If you are not gettin' any then comfort food is a good back up. Men really should sharpen up. What the hell do they think is sexy about eating unhealthily and being massively overweight? What is it that makes even the most shambolic of men think they stand a chance with any woman who works hard at her appearance to stay fit, healthy, and attractive to the opposite sex? The male chutzpah is never to be underestimated. (Ok rant over – back to the job in hand).

The world is full of single men, but you may well have to compromise. Except if they don't like dogs and you do. NEVER compromise on that. The relationship really won't work.

So go ahead. Imagine what it is you are looking for.

## Georgia 37

Here's my little story. I was so busy running my business I didn't have time to find love. Then one day love marched right up to me.

15 years ago I was a waitress. Probably a good one too. Then one day I decided to take a cooking course. I qualified as a chef and started my own business. I was mainly providing canapes for parties, business lunches, cooking for dinner parties etc. Doing all the ordering, cooking, and delivering myself and hiring in teams of waiting staff when needed and eventually business grew successfully. But it wasn't a straightforward start. It was hard to get going. My first business came from friends who recommended me. I got one catering contract from a friend who ran a creative advertising agency. The company were producing a music video for a famous rock group and the shoot was taking place in a converted warehouse in south London. I was contracted to provide a simple lunch. All they wanted was Lasagne, salad, garlic bread, fruit, oh and a special request for peas. All very simple. I would be catering for 40 people made up of the film crew, the rock group, models, actors, and managers. It was nothing big, but it would get me started. It was my first contract and of course it was important to me.

The day before the film shoot, I collected all the ingredients and went back to the kitchen to prepare and cook all the food for the next day. I shared a house with a friend who worked in a PR agency and was out most of the day. The friend was quite a party girl, so she was usually out most of the evening as well. I wasn't expecting to see her and we often passed like ships in the night. Occasionally we would catch up at the weekend.

By 9pm that night I'd finished making all the lasagne. There were three large catering dishes ready to be reheated the next day. It looked and smelt good. Anyone who has ever eaten cold lasagne can know how good it can taste. Closing the light in the kitchen, I went to bed early leaving the lasagne cooling on the counter. Going upstairs to my bedroom it wasn't long before I fell into a deep sleep. I didn't hear my housemate come in three hours later. Nor did I hear the group of friends and dropouts from the nightclub that arrived as well. This was nearly 1am, and this group of people were stoned, drunk and hungry. They ate my lasagne.

I got up at 7am and saw that out of the three dishes of lasagne one had been eaten and the other dug into with forks and partly eaten. I was really panicking. I did the only thing I could. I set about making more lasagne. First there was the shopping and again the food prep but by 11am I had made two new lasagne dishes and was now heading with the help of a friend to the warehouse in southeast London with trays of lasagne, salad, peas, and garlic bread. Nothing else could possibly go wrong but of course it did. I was by now stressed from this morning and exhausted. As I carried the dish of peas to the top of the stairs in the studio, I dropped it. The peas rolled down the stairs. A bright green cascade of little petit pois. As no one saw me and thinking I was alone, I scooped up the peas and started putting them back into the dish as fast as I could. I was bent down doing this and so didn't realise immediately that someone was helping me. I looked up and saw that a tall, skinny, handsome man was laughing and scooping peas off the stair and into the dish. I didn't know who he was, but I was grateful – and embarrassed. So I said thank you, grabbed the dish and ran off in the direction of the dining area.

I remember that as I laid out the lunch I could hear the sound coming from the studio. I recognised the track they were filming to. The band was a well-known rock group but I was not particularly a fan of their type of music, although I certainly knew who the band was. Other than that I didn't think further about it - too busy setting out dishes and making sure the lasagne stayed hot. I washed the peas so there was no visible carpet fluff or general grit from the stairwell. Phew! They looked OK.

The music stopped and shortly after people started arriving for lunch – helping themselves to lasagne, salad and …. peas. The band strolled in surrounded by managers and hangers on. I recognised the guy who had helped with the peas. He was the lead singer of the band – and when he helped himself to lunch, he made a point of asking for extra peas and winked at me. That wasn't the end of it. When I was clearing up he came over to talk to me. Somehow, we got into a conversation about windmills and how he'd stayed in one recently. In Norfolk. This is where I am from. So I was happy to have that relaxing conversation. But it was one of those chats that somehow two

*Delissa Needham*

people get lost in and forget where they are or who else is around. I suddenly felt there were just the two of us in the room. It was weird. He asked me to have a drink with him later. And that was 'our beginning'.

Remember. Anytime, anywhere – it can happen anyhow.

## Chapter Eighteen

## DATING IN THE REAL WORLD IS FUN.

All this dating malarkey is meant to be fun. Enjoy it. When you're left nursing a broken heart, holding a baby, sawing the dog in half etc then you're allowed to think well that didn't work out right, so I'll have a good cry. But the girl who intends to meet a man doesn't fall at the first fence unless she's had one too many tequila shots.

*Chapter Nineteen*

# RECAP: LET'S GO OVER THAT AGAIN.

A reminder of some important thinking…

Be realistic.

There are a lot of single women out there.

You need to focus and act strategically. Imagine you are in a crowded bar of other single women of all ages. You need to fight your way through them all to get to the front – to the bar – to get the barman's attention. Jostling at the bar with lots of other women.

Think of that metaphor and you will picture the extent of the competition. That means you must:

Look your best.

Be outstanding.

Smile.

Charm.

Keep your eyes open.

Network – don't rely on friends.

Plan.

Focus.

Don't leave it to chance.

Be interesting and be interested. Learn to listen.

Learn the art of conversation – avoid boring clichés.

Ask interesting questions.

AND most importantly – have a strategy. One that isn't based on hanging out in clubs and bars with other single women.

I know this seems a tall order, but you can practise whilst you are going about your daily business until it becomes second nature. You never know, it may just improve the quality of your neighbourhood. Make eye contact with the cashier in the supermarket. Greet your neighbour, smile at the receptionist. Not so scary really.

## DON'T PROJECT

So suppose you have met someone.

*Delissa Needham*

Now what? Well firstly don't project. If you are the kind of person that can't meet a man for a coffee without immediately planning the wedding, then woah – back up lady. Oh alright go on, let's have two minutes of wedding planning. What style of dress are you wearing? What colour? Really? Are you sure that suits you? Got the guest list sorted, the food planned, the venue decided… there's just one thing missing… oh yeah, the groom!

Don't project. It just means you start stepping away from reality and start muddying the water with what you think he is and can't see what he really is. Look for what he is – not what you want him to be. Just because someone seems to be a wonderful man doesn't mean he is. Don't take it to heart when friends all think he is terrific. They want the best for you. Look for yourself - don't listen to your mother, your best friend etc.

Love isn't love until it's had the test of time and you've had the time to get to know someone, otherwise it's just a sex fest – and that's terribly confusing.

You can only know what a man is really like based on how well he treats you and others. A good lasting relationship is not about status or power, it's about a set of characteristics that you admire and a code of behaviour that is not selective but treats all with the same moral code.

Projecting is also a slippery slope to putting your eggs in one basket. That way you'll be so disappointed, and even more heart broken if it doesn't work out. So really - don't rush it.

And remember – don't be too available – you may lose value that way.

It's all too easy when a man feels he's pushing an open door for boredom to set in. A man likes to hunt – he'll just step over the deer that lies down and dies.

Nobody deserves your entire focus until you have a real relationship with them based on real values – honesty, kindness, loyalty etc. You need to keep exploring and keep your options open until you decide, yes, this is the one. And then and only then do you give it your exclusive attention – because only then when you've decided it's worth it.

Don't start ignoring your friends and other possible partners until you are sure you are with the right man. Move slowly, observe carefully, don't rush in with your eyes shut. And chances are if you move slowly, he will move quickly. There's nothing like a dame dragging her heels hesitantly for a man to wonder 'why – what's wrong with me? Why is she not making a commitment?'. Likely then he will try harder.

By the same token be wary of how he sees you. It's easy to project onto a man all the things you want him to be and ignoring what he really is and by the same thinking it's also easy for a man to project onto you what he wants you to be. Is he falling in love with what he thinks you are? Not what you really are.

Widows and widowers are particularly susceptible to that kind of projection. Happily married for many years, they think all subsequent partners will be the same as the departed spouse. But when the dog dies and you get a new dog, same breed but new dog, do you think it will be the same as the dog that's passed away? No. It's a new dog. Different behaviours and different habits etc. People are all very different. You cannot hope to replace what you had with more of the same.

Both people in a relationship need to invest slowly and carefully in each other. Only when you have both put time and effort into it will it begin to seem valuable and real. You both need to work at it to value each other. And it's worth remembering that just because a man says he loves you … doesn't mean he wants to spend the rest of his life with you. To achieve that takes time for both of you. We women know that it's important to feel that our man cares for and cherishes us. Not just empty compliments but words matched by behaviour and thought.

You see once you have met the right man. That isn't the end. It's not the end even when he makes a commitment. It's only the beginning of everything. Once you meet that right man the work goes on. You need to work just as hard at keeping the man as you did at finding him in the first place. You gotta keep watering the plants, basting the turkey, trimming the hedge, having a Brazilian. If you decide that this is the right man for you then you need to keep working at it only then will it bring the rewards that a happy relationship can bring. Two people together enjoying each other's company – nurturing each other, caring for each other. Having your own passions and interests as well as having ones that you share. A relationship is a two-way street. You gotta keep the traffic flowing.

You may feel you know what you need from a man (plus a dress, a venue, and a suggestion for the first dance) but have you thought about what he needs. Here's a very generalised list.

The ego – it needs to be nurtured. (Buy more jars of pickles).

He needs to feel cared for. Special. (So knit him some socks).

Loyalty, friendship, support. (Just like you get in any department store).

So be on his team. Be a friend.

Men are providers but as we move into older relationships most single women have already provided for themselves, thereby removing the old fashioned but traditional role of 'provider' away from the man. That's still a relatively new situation for some men, depending on their age. It can impact on the balance of a relationship with some men being in awe of it and others feeling threatened by it. So to reiterate my previous chapter, do be a strong woman but do be feminine. Of course you are free to have an 'attitude' and team it with some ugly army boots, but then if you do that, the man you attract may not be what you wanted. And finding the man you do want to attract will be like looking for a needle in a haystack. You will have to hope that your ideal man is going to fall for some hidden feminine trait that you are keeping in your baggy camouflage pants.

It's a mistake to be more of a man than a man is? He's not looking to fall in love with his own sex - your ideal man is looking to fall in love with a woman, a feminine woman. So hang up your ugly heavy boots and be a woman. Not a mirror image of a man. Weird notion.

This lovely story of how two people met was told to me by Mary before she went to live in the care home where she died during lockdown. The love of her life, constant companion and friend, her husband Bill was not allowed to be with her. I'll let her words tell it. It's a beautiful story.

## Mary 91

We've known each other nearly all our lives. As distant cousins we met first at a family gathering when I was six and Bill was seven. We were on the same team for a game of rounders in Aunt Joan's Garden. It had been the start of a summer in which Bill and his gang of friends had allowed me to accompany them on their many adventures in the fields at the back of Joan's house. Bill lived next door with my other aunt, Margaret. Bill lived with his four older brothers and his parents. I had come to stay for the summer while my mother recuperated from a medical procedure. I was an only child so to have Bill and his friends to play with – and my older cousins was fun. Bill looked after me from day one. Never having had a sister, I was the focus of his attention, caring for me. When I fell out of the apple tree and grazed my knee it was Bill who wiped my tears, helped me home, washed my knee and applied the stinging iodine and then a plaster. And it was Bill that took

*How I Met My Man and How You Can Meet Yours*

it off a week later. That hurt more than the graze. When Bill's dog was hit by a car it was me that Bill wanted to talk to. When Bill passed his exams and went off to university it was me he rushed home to see at half term and holidays. Whilst we both got on with our lives – meeting other people, making friends, forging careers – it was still always 'us'. Bill and Mary. I always knew – so did Bill. It took him a little longer to realise – after all he was a man. He dated a few other women while at university – away from my sight. Maybe he did that on purpose – the Universe having already decided what was the right thing for Bill and he maybe just wanted to be sure. And it was the right thing. When he finished university for good, he landed a job as an engineer with a company just outside London. It was over 150 miles away from his home town and Bill was excited about starting a new job. He found a place to live and started work. But he called me every single day on the phone and came home on weekends. We just wanted to be together. Life was nothing without Bill. Shortly before he was promoted with a job to take up in Hong Kong, Bill proposed to me. He was 23 and I was 22. I said yes and we started our married life together just a few months later. Our first child, a boy, was born a year after our wedding day and in quick succession two other children were born just a year apart. Bill had bandaged my knee when I was six and he went on bandaging my knee throughout our lives together. Our son died aged just nine. No parent expects to bury a child and I do believe that only our love for each other and our shared religious faith enabled us to come to terms with what happened. Our son Tom was swimming with his friends in a nearby lake and got tangled in the weeds. The strong undercurrent dragged him down. When they pulled up the body Bill had to identify him. Only love has helped us cope. We had our children and many grandchildren and eventually even great grandchildren. Our marriage and our love for each other never dimmed.

*** 

Bill was not able to be with Mary when she died alone. She had been his great love since he was just a boy of seven. He didn't want to live without her and just a week later he lay down and died. He went to bed in their family home and just simply didn't wake up.

# PART 5:
# AND FINALLY...

*Chapter Twenty*

# FOR THE 35's AND UNDER

This chapter is specifically for 'youth'. Those in the 'marrying' bracket. You are in the land of plenty. Because that's what it is.

A dad was telling me recently that he was worried that his daughter who is 25 and beautiful wants to meet a boy and fall in love, but she hardly goes out and doesn't meet anyone when she does. Many of her friends are sleeping around but this is not what she wants. So now she is looking on the internet to meet someone. She is using online dating and still not meeting anyone.

It happens to everyone no matter their age.

Why is that? How can that be?

Let me ask you a question. A question you will be asked many times in your career and a question you will ask yourself (or should about your job).

*How I Met My Man and How You Can Meet Yours*

Where do you want to be in 10 years' time? That question dictates what you do in your job now. Right now.

Perhaps you've decided that you'd like to keep working your way up the career ladder, with salary increases, promotions etc, pay off your mortgage and retire at 50 to enjoy the second home you bought in the Med etc.

So you look around you – assess the company you are with and decide whether this is the right place for you to achieve what you want long term.

You do that with your career. So why don't you do that with your boyfriend?

When you start job hunting you are looking at the company you might join and wondering how they fit into your future.

If you don't do that with a relationship, then you'll end up having more than one expensive wedding. So unless you like white dresses now is the time to plan ahead. Look to the future and decide what you want.

Where do you see yourself in your married life at 60? Who do you want to retire with?

Who do you want to be the father of your children?

Who do you want to be in your life for the rest of your life?

You think that sounds calculating? No, it's thinking about your future. You think men don't do that? Yes, they do. Men are looking for the mother of their children as well as their partner for life.

Do you want to be able to have a conversation over the breakfast marmalade or do you want to sit in silence in restaurants in your retirement, bored stiff because neither of you have anything to say to each other?

So what are the characteristics that matter most to you? What do you want your life partner to be like?Kind, intelligent, hard working. This thinking will influence getting off your bum with a strategy for your future marital/relationship happiness.

In an earlier chapter I described how a friend advised me on how to decide where I wanted to live. Where I wanted to move to. *"What do you want"*, she said. *"Think about how you want to spend each hour of the day"*. I said I wanted to walk the dog, to be able to take my laptop to a café, to be able to get to London quickly, to be around people daily. That eye on my future life defined my location to live. Rather than just grabbing the prettiest cottage I found, instead I thought about how I wanted to be on a day to day basis.

Look at your own situation in your second or third decade of life. You are in the marriage market age bracket. Its rich pickings. Everyone is on the start line looking for someone to be with.

So <u>how</u> do you want that person to be? How do you see your existence together when you are say 45? Imagine your kids are now at Uni or working. Would you like to think that your husband gets up in the morning and goes for a healthy run? Eats a healthy breakfast and then leaves for a job and a career he works hard at? After work is done, he plays football, rugby, cricket etc. Maybe he walks the dog. You have shared friends and shared interests. Maybe you play tennis together or have separate friends, interests, passions, and sports. Perhaps he's passionate about something that really interests him like history, travel etc. He has a life outside his job. Is this man practical, do you want him to be handy and clever at doing things, from being able to fix the shelf on the wall to building you a new home.

Do you want your husband to have friends, mates he meets down the pub. Friends he talks to and does things with? Good friendships are healthy.

Do you want a partner to be someone you can enjoy life with? Of course you do. Think about how you see your relationship and your marriage and who it is that fits that role.

In other words do you want a life together that is packed. Do you want him to be someone who will work alongside you to build a future together for you and your children? Look towards the end point – look down the line.

What do you want your life to be? How do you see yourself in 20 years?

Then ask yourself what the man who you want to have your projected future life with at 45 and onwards is doing right now.

I'm not judging here but…..well here comes the judgement….

*Delissa Needham*

Is the man you envisage sitting behind a computer looking online for a girlfriend? Or is he out there getting on with life. Doing sports, meeting friends, building something, tinkering with an old car, making a shelf. Is he mud running for charity this weekend or at rugby practice on Saturday morning? Maybe he keeps bees, plays the drums in his spare time with a band, reads the lesson at his local church, brews beer, has an ecology system in his backyard….. I don't know; I'm just pulling thoughts out of a hat. All I'm saying is your future with a man who is out there right now doing things. Being active and busy in the world. Making new friends and in the process meeting girls. Whether that girl is in his rowing club or at the bar in the local pub. His social life and therefore his dating life is not on a screen.

The man sitting at the computer online dating is being lazy, In my view. You are in the marriage market bracket. You are young. You have energy. Get out there.

What you start with is pretty much what you end up with.

Remember what happens when you order your groceries online? It's better to get off your bum and go to the shop yourself. The apple you pick will be better than the one the supermarket stacker picked. Go pick your own - or leave it to the algorithms who might not choose the best apple for you.

## Amanda

It's really weird how I met my husband but so typical of the time. So typical of being young and having a great time. I was

195

in my late 20's and having a wild time. Everyone was looking for someone. I was that age when you are part having fun but also wanting to meet that special person that you just might end up marrying. I was partying like there was no tomorrow and holding down the day job in PR. There were many times I drove to work topping up last night's make-up in my rear-view mirror, with one eye on the road and the other on my lipstick. Crazy! How did I survive?

One night I went to a party with my flatmate. It was one of those parties in someone's house with great music, plenty of drinks, and lots of dark corners. Somehow, I ended up kissing this guy. We were talking and I noticed his lips and remembered thinking I want to kiss them. So I did. We spent the rest of the night kissing. In a corner. Snogging and giggling. I never got his name. I never asked. Sometime after midnight my flatmate dragged me off into a black cab and home. Next day I was at my desk with a black coffee and a hangover, and my flatmate rang. The girl who had the party had rung her to say that one of her friends brought a guy with her who had spent all night kissing a girl and never got her name.

He'd like to see her again – did I want him to have my number? Why not? He rang me at work, and we had a short chat and he arranged to pick me up two weeks later. Why so far away. Because that's how things worked then. We didn't have mobile phones, so everything was sorted diary wise for at least two weeks ahead. My schedule usually went like this.

Monday – cinema with friends. Tuesday was usually a night for an activity like tennis or netball. Wednesday was dinner at someone's house – or at mine. At mine it was always the same menu. Cucumber soup (easy as all you do is whizz up a cucumber and yoghurt), followed by Spag Bol and salad, then ice cream. You could do all that in 30 mins max. Thursday was a date night in a pub or restaurant. Friday was a party night or leave London to stay with friends in the country. So when The Snogger rang it was two weeks before I saw him again.

I remember I was zipping up my dress when the doorbell rang. Bang on 7.30. Whoever arrives on time?? It's so rude!! Grrr!!! I wrenched the door open and this guy is standing there. Average height - a city boy haircut, nice jeans, a great shirt, and a jacket with a flashy lining. Nice smile, good teeth. Hm! I'd done well in that dark corner. We exchanged a few ordinary pleasantries. Nervously actually and then we went down to his car. It was a green jag XJ which was kind of weird because I went out with a guy the week before who also drove a green jag XJ. I'd had too much to drink then and thrown up over the inside of it, so this was definitely not the same car. He was fun company. Really made me laugh and we were having one of those conversations where it just feels like there's the two of you. He was so interesting and more than that... so interested. He asked questions about me. Wanted to know what I thought of this or that. I was having the loveliest time. Then something suddenly occurred to me. This was not the guy I had been snogging at that party. Ooooh, should I say something. While I was part listening and part pondering the dilemma, he suddenly looked at me and said it out loud. The same thing I was thinking. It wasn't me, was it? We both realised we'd never met before, and he'd realised that when I answered the door but didn't want to say it. It didn't matter anyway. Somewhere in a parallel universe two people who were snogging at a party might have ended up with each other – or not. Who cares? We did. Phillipe and I have been together for 35 years.

## Chapter Twenty One

## STUFF FOR YOU TO THINK ABOUT

*How I Met My Man* is a book to encourage you. To make you realise that you can and must do something proactive if you want to meet someone. There are plenty of people like you in the same situation, so there is someone out there for you. I know because I speak to them as clients. Widowers, divorcees, singletons etc. People looking for someone. But clients tell me they are lonely, and I ask what they are doing about it, usually it boils down to … nothing. THINKING about joining the tennis club. THINKING about joining a golf club, or local am dram, or Bridge etc. Do you have time for such procrastination? If you are lonely and if you want to meet someone special then you must get off your bottom, open the door and go out. All the thinking that you need to do is to focus on what you want, who you are and where you can go to find what you are looking for. A lady in her 70's told me the other day she was new in town and didn't know anyone but was thinking of joining a golf club. It sounded as though the thinking had taken the place of activity for quite some time. There are five golf clubs in her busy town. Go look, I said, and see which club most suits what you want. Don't go on a Saturday because your kind of man is not a working man. He is more likely to be retired. So go look at golf clubs on weekdays in mid-morning.

You don't need money to meet people. Volunteer for something. Guiding around historic buildings will put you in touch with a team and visitors. Look at the 'what's on' guide for your town and decide what's going to be enjoyable so you don't waste your enthusiasm.

Three summers ago I took the hour-long train ride from my home into London. I rode to the station on my bike and loaded it onto the train. I was wearing a noticeable green jumpsuit and as I sat down an older lady across the aisle exclaimed with delight that she'd seen me cycling through the town 'like a flash of green'. She was very chatty. We spoke about so many different things. Who were her favourite actors? What books she liked. Who do I like reading? Had I been to Southwark Cathedral? It was a very interesting and lively conversation. When other people got on the train, she also engaged them in conversation. She said to one man how much she liked his yellow striped jumper and hoped it didn't mean he could sting like a bee. When we arrived in Charing Cross, I said goodbye and asked where she was going in London. Oh I'm just going to the end of the line was her reply. She takes the train so she can meet people. So she can talk to people. How extraordinary is that? So here is a lady who was obviously feeling lonely and decided to do something about it. Unlike you she wasn't looking for love or a partner. She just wanted company. And she had an unusual but successful way of finding it.

I know that the hardest thing about looking for love, hoping to meet somebody new etc is that, unlike when you look online, you need confidence. Bags of it. Bottom line is that you need enough courage to go up to strangers at a party and say hello. Just remember that if you are genuinely interested enough then people are happy to talk to you.

Like my lovely client Marianne who was invited to a party where she didn't know anyone other than the host. It's a daunting proposition and especially for a recently divorced woman in her 60's. It's enough to make another night in front of the telly look quite appealing. And that was her preference, but we talked about it. Marianne had promised the host she would go, and besides, if you really want to meet someone then you will have to jump some difficult fences. And as you will know from a previous chapter my favourite mantra is 'turn up'. You can always leave if you really hate it. Firstly, it's important to turn up late rather than early if you don't know anyone. Marianne entered the room 45 minutes late by which time the other party goers were quite lubricated and easier to say hello to. She asked a nearby male guest to pass her a glass of champagne, which he did, and they got talking. He introduced her to someone else and so on. Then lo and behold an old boyfriend from 30 years ago appeared. When she left that evening, she had four business cards in her bag and a date for coffee the following week. Is there a trick to that? Not really. Marianne was just being interested in people and participating in interesting conversations. You don't get that sitting on a sofa.

So whatever you may have gleaned from this book, I hope what sticks is that you must be proactive, focussed, gutsy, feminine, and always looking your best. The more you meet people the more you will meet more people. Until you too meet the man of your dreams and the story of how you met joins modern day folklore. Good luck!

Printed in Great Britain
by Amazon